Wild Women Make the Best Leaders

A Guide to Embracing the Untamed Spirit for Fierce Leadership

Shanna Parmley

Contents

Introduction

Wild women make the best leaders. It's more than just the title of this book—it's an absolute fact about the world around us that more people could do with knowing. Wild women run the world, leading with confidence, innovation, tact, a pinch of grace, and a lot of passion. Wild women are those who never learned to quiet down, who embraced their "too much"-ness and became a more empowered version of themselves.

Leading can be a daunting task for a woman who isn't wild. It can feel like you're going to be shut down or that you never know what to say. Leadership positions can be scary when it seems like a male-dominated force or everyone expects you to be curt. The fabulous news is that *any* woman can learn to embrace their inner wild.

This book is the secret to embracing the hectic entanglement of your personality and becoming a better leader than ever. Inside, you will find everything you need, whether you already love your inner wildness or seek to begin the journey today. You'll uncover

- the myth of perfection: Why perfection doesn't always mean that someone is the best leader, and how your imperfections make you flawless as a leader.

- how to find a voice that screams, yells, and stands up for itself—the voice inside of you that doesn't ask for permission.

- wild vs. reckless: Understand how you can take calculated risks while embracing your truly wild nature.

- developing resilience, a support network, and confidence.

Being a wild woman isn't something to tamp down; it's something to love yourself for. The fact of the matter is that the world needs more wild women. With compassion, a touch of humor, and overarching themes of loving who you are, this book helps you navigate everything you need to change boardrooms and meetings alike.

I'll let you in on a secret: Wild women make the best leaders because we care so intensely and with such an unparalleled fervor. Your passion is what makes you who you are, and you should *never* have to suppress that! With that being said, it's time to set forth on this journey to embracing your wild nature once and for all. Every woman has one—we just have to tease her out!

Without further ado, let's get started and empower each other for a life of wild, radiant beauty in leadership. A chain reaction of wild women begins with you!

Chapter 1:

The Wild Woman—Myth, Legend,

Boss

If you are always trying to be normal, you'll never know how amazing you can be. –
Maya Angelou

Being a wild woman is not just about being a woman who happens to be wild. In fact, being a wild woman is something you embody. It is an established concept and archetype that you can learn more about, harnessing what it truly means to be wild *and* embrace that wildness with rebellion, joy, and a touch of grace for balance. In this chapter, you will dive into what it means to be a wild woman in the truest sense of the phrase, meaning that by the end of this chapter, nothing will tamp down your unparalleled inner fire.

The Wild Woman Archetype

Besides being an outspoken and radiant boss of a woman, what does it really mean to be a wild woman? We can understand the role of the wild woman by taking a look at the wild woman archetype. By doing so, you hone a magnificent understanding of what it means to truly embrace the inner storm that makes you the more resilient, vibrant version of who you can be!

Wild women are more than a myth or a stereotype. Wild women are found in real life in offices and other occupations, in media and film, and even within the dynamics of a single family. The wild woman is something that has only been given a name recently, yet she has been here all along, perhaps since the inception of time itself.

Wild women are dynamic and rebellious. Cognitive psychology insists that wild women are instinctive beings who have a natural tenacity for that inner wildness. Some think that being a wild woman equates to embracing sexuality, while others feel that a wild woman is any lady with drive and ambition bursting from her seams. If you ask me, being a wild woman is all of the above and none of it at the same time.

The prevailing undercurrent of the wild woman archetype is that she's self-made, confident, and exactly who she is meant to be—comfortable in her own skin. If that means embracing sexuality to you, then that is what makes you wild; if being wild is about screaming your passions from the mountain tops (or standing up for them from a seat at the office meeting table), then that is your personal meaning of wild.

According to the wild woman archetype, we are also magnifications of other feminine archetypes. Other archetypes surrounding women posit that we are nurturing, wise, maternal, or empathetic. In my book, a wild woman can radiate particular elements of every other archetype depending on her goals and unique qualities—and the wild woman archetype agrees! This is why no two wild women are exactly the same, yet *every* wild woman is someone to behold.

Much like it is difficult to put your finger on just what makes a wild woman who she is, it is also difficult to pin down what it is that makes the wild woman archetype so catalyzing and fabulous all at the same time. Wild women as an archetype are often the women who do not "fit" anywhere else; we are not simply wise or quiet, domineering or passionate. We dance between the interlocking components of who a woman can be, stereotypes, rarities, and all.

No matter who you ask, the wild woman archetype is going to be different. What rings true about all wild women, however, is that they shout "no" in the face of conformity; if society tries to force you to be someone you are not, then you reject it wholeheartedly. No social expectation could be as glamorous as what makes you, well, you!

To sum it up, wild women are fiercely unpredictable and uncontrollable beings. We do not bend to the will of others, nor do we shove down who we are as a compromise to someone's opinion. Wild women are like kaleidoscopes, truly forming the best of both worlds when it comes to the dichotomy of women. And best of all? Anyone can learn to be a wild, infallible woman *if* you know the tricks of the trade!

Women Have Always Run Things!

Since the dawn of time, women have been running things, especially where no one else could. Wild women especially have mastered taking the wheel, whether it comes to leadership, family, or even survival, as early as ancient times. By taking a look at how women have always run things, it becomes easy to empower yourself and realize that you truly can do anything that you set your mind to!

Ancient Civilization

Women have been running things forever, and ancient times are no exception. While men have had an undeniable part in history, women have always played unique roles in making ends meet, ensuring family satisfaction, and keeping everyone happy *and* healthy. Depending on the class of one's family, women carried out different roles—many of which are actually not dissimilar from the stereotypical roles people expect us to carry out today.

For example, women in lower-class families carried out many specific duties. A lot of women spun and wove clothing, which is a pretty fascinating and admirable task. I mean, making clothes from something like a ball of yarn is no easy feat. Maternal instincts also led to the role of ancient women in caring for a family, especially the children. Many women in ancient households were in charge of running the home itself, with men taking on tasks like hunting and manual labor. Equal and opposite duties, one might say.

But to go back even further, there were societies that were characterized by hunter/gatherer dynamics. This referred to the fact that some members of society would hunt for game and big animals—which would then be turned into food, weapons, clothing, and more—while others foraged and collected necessities from the earth. For many societies, women were the gatherers.

This led to the fact that women had a very intimate knowledge of how the Earth worked. Gathering women were wild in the purest form, aligning themselves with seasonal cycles, medicinal wisdom, and more to support their family and village from the very soil we appreciate today. Women were not just considered to be homemakers; they were beholders of sacred wisdom, too.

Moreover, certain societies viewed women as sacred in and of themselves. The female body is what produces life. Entire human beings come from the female body, and that is not to mention the other life-sustaining functions a woman's body can carry out. Many cultures perceived women and female functions to be as sacred as the Earth itself, leading to a deep reverence and respect.

With that being said, women were not idle beings during ancient times. We ran households with all the authority of military commanders; we treated the Earth like a piece of ourselves as we used it to sustain not just families but entire societies. Women have always run things in a unique and unparalleled manner that is undeniably present, even today.

Women in Household Settings

When someone thinks of a woman, there is still the ingrained stereotype that women are homemakers, which in part does originate from ancient times. People think women are more adept at cooking, cleaning, raising kids, and so on, even to the point that it becomes a harmful stereotype. And while it is not okay to force anyone into the tiny box of a gender role, I think this expectation of women speaks to one of our glaring historical successes.

That is, women are known for boss-like leadership in household settings because we are truly that good at it. Women have empathy for others in a way no one else can truly understand. We experience pain, suffering, emotions, and even needs, unlike men, which means that we can often find more connection to other living beings, including women, children, and animals.

Furthermore, there are countless studies that suggest that women have a better aptitude for certain details, including intricacies. This means that we excel at tasks in ways no one else can match. In a household alone, one woman can play the role of

- **Mother:** Even without kids, a woman can be a mother. Mothering refers to giving something life, which means one can nurture a child, pet, or passion. Being a mother means something different to everyone, and it is something unique to women.

- **Chef:** Making cuisine and mastering the art of meal preparation is something a lot of women excel at. It goes beyond cooking into the bliss of creation, plating, presentation, and sharing memories over a warm meal.

- **Cleaner:** Some of the best cleaners I know are women, which is because we are intuitive, attentive, and love a space that makes us feel amazing. And besides, wild women know that you can be clean and a little cluttered, making that house feel like a home.

- **Interior designer:** Decorating is a wonderful hobby that many wild women love. It is like transforming your inner landscape into something others can perceive. Whether that expression is in the form of a carefully polished, intentional living room or a vibrantly clashing, chaotically loved bedroom, a wild woman is the one to show you what design is all about.

- **Therapist:** Wild women are not inconsiderate women. Wild women know what it's like to have our emotions negated, which is why we are perfect for your rants, venting, and even offering advice that nurtures your inner peace.

- **Negotiator:** At the same time, a wild woman is not afraid to fight and swim against the current, coming to compromises that are truly fair or asserting herself for what she knows is right.

- **Teacher:** We make the best teachers because we intertwine experience with knowledge. This means that in a home, women also serve as educators!

- **Role model:** Best of all, a wild woman in a home shows everyone what it is like to take no nonsense and embrace yourself and who you are!

And that is just the start of it!

Women in Leadership Positions

Women do not just exist inside the home; in fact, breaking free from the stereotype that women are homebodies is a good thing! That is why it is so important to understand that women, especially wild ones, can be profound leaders who do a better job than anyone else you put to the task. And I'm not just saying that—there is evidence supporting this line of thinking as well.

For instance, one analysis of over 60 studies of women in leadership proved that women are able to be more transformative with their leadership (Novotney, 2023). This means that women are more likely to take an overview of what is best for an organization as a whole before acting, leading to better outcomes for the entire establishment.

In addition, women excel at all of the skills needed to be good leaders, especially compared to male leaders. Some of the most fundamental skills needed to be a good leader include emotional intelligence, listening, creativity, and empathy (Agaragimova, 2022). Not only are women 9% more likely to exhibit a positive outlook and emotional intelligence than men in the same leadership positions, but we are also 45% more likely to display consistent streams of empathy in a work environment (*New Research Shows Women Are Better at Using Soft Skills*, n.d.).

What that means is that whether a woman is leading a small team or a Fortune 500 company, she has the ability to excel in ways that her male counterparts might not. Considering wild women in particular, the skills of ambition, pushing the limits, and innovation are also heightened, leading to the perfect blend of emotional consideration and risk-taking for a successful leader.

Social Barriers to Being Wild: How Society Works Against You

Unfortunately, modern society comes locked and loaded with countless ways to restrict wild women. From the dawn of time, society has been telling us that we are too loud, too crazy, or too dominant, and it is time to break down that barrier and make wild women the *expectation*. At the same time, it is helpful to know exactly what you are up against when it comes to fighting the suppression of wild women!

Stereotype 1: Women Should be Submissive

Even if someone does not outwardly admit it, there's a prevalent undercurrent within our society that pushes the expectation of submissiveness onto women. The fact of the matter is that we are not born submissive. There's nothing wrong with a woman who chooses to be submissive, but for the vast majority of women, it is not a choice. So, why are women thought to be submissive in the first place?

There are a few reasons why this stereotype is so pervasive:

- Certain Western ideals believed women to be weak and incapable due to their period or other natural bodily functions.

- Men were frequently the subject of scientific studies, not women, thus leading to the idea that most female "problems" were mental and not a reflection of physical health or her environment.

- Female hysteria took hold in medical circles and pushed the idea that women who did not have enough sex eventually went crazy, among other things, positing us as submissive sexual beings.

- Female submission paved the road to men being dominant and domineering, and because men had more time to be in charge of running society while women were having children, men got the first say.

Many other reasons factor in as well. Women are not any more "naturally" submissive than men are; it falls to the fact that women are encouraged to be submissive—while men are told that their own submissiveness should be suppressed—as to why women *seem* submissive. And prevailing submissiveness stereotypes are only enforced by blind sexism and the refusal to think critically by many.

Stereotype 2: Women Belong in the Kitchen

There is this saying that "women belong in the kitchen," highlighting the fact that traditional women took over such a role. Today, that phrase is used to confine women to boxes that they do not want to crouch within. If you've been fortunate enough to have never heard this phrase, it is often used to say that women should be cooking and not trying to have a say.

While we are capable of producing some fabulous food, there is nothing biological that says we are any better suited for the kitchen than a man is. The mere idea that men should not cook or clean stems from patriarchal standards, not from research and data. In fact, there is no research suggesting that women have a higher propensity for kitchen duties—definitely a total shock to hear that as a woman, right?

Stereotype 3: Women are Too Emotional

Nine times out of ten, if you ask a man what he finds to be the worst quality in women, he's going to say that we are too emotional.

Countless research and studies have proven that we are not more emotional; however, we are better at intelligently expressing and communicating our emotions. If anything, the stereotype that women are too emotional just shows that men have been forced—both by their own hand and the efforts of others—to avoid intelligent, emotional expression. Why do they think emotional ignorance and disconnect are something to brag about?

How to Overcome Gender Bias Against Women: A Brief Overview

Of course, those three stereotypes are far from everything that afflicts a modern wild woman, but they do provide a look at how many of those stereotypes are nonsense—they lack a scientific basis for their logic, which means they usually come from prejudice and close-mindedness. Still, they influence me and you every single day. What can we do about it?

As a woman, you have a lot of options when it comes to overcoming the gender bias that we face. While it can be as simple as refusing to buy things just because they are pink or feeling like you need to wear a dress, it also has to do with education. Both participating in and spreading education regarding women and women's rights, health, and welfare can make a big difference when it comes to how women are perceived within society.

Moreover, correcting people in their casual streams of sexism is a wonderful way to make wild women feel more welcome. Subtle workplace undermining or sexualization of women, for instance, is always something that you can speak up against. And when you speak up for women, others will feel empowered to do the same. This also comes in the form of refusing to do something for someone just because they assume you will due to your gender.

It is also important that you play a role in encouraging men to feel comfortable with their more "feminine" side; allow men to have a safe space to express and explore emotions, contribute to more gentle approaches, and engage with tasks you might typically assign to women. A significant part of anti-woman bias comes from the fact that men have a rooted fear of "girly" things, so try to make it known that something like an emotion, article of clothing, or color has no gender.

And best of all, you can embrace your inner wild. Men do not anticipate a woman to be so unforgiving in her authenticity, passion, and personal freedom, but when you take steps to shout in the face of the world that "I am not afraid to be myself," you set the standard that women do not have to be neat little housekeepers. We are wild and dangerous if tempted, and that is a beautiful thing. By showing society that you know just how powerful you are as a wild woman, those stereotypes crumble one day at a time.

Chapter Activity: What Wild Means to You

What does wild mean to you? Do not just mull it over—journal about it! Using the space below, describe what it means to you to be wild. You can consider questions like

- What does it mean for me to be wild?

- What is stopping me from being wild?

- How would my life change if I embraced being wild?

_____

_____

_____

_____

_____

_____

_____

_____

_____

_____

_____

_____

_____

_____

_____

_____

_____

_____

Being a wild woman does not mean that you are off the wall, irresponsible, or immature; in fact, now you know exactly what it means to be a wild woman and exactly what role wild women have been playing in society for centuries. With that being said, it is time to shift our lens to understanding perfection, including the idea that women have to be "perfect" in order to be good leaders.

Chapter 2:

Not a Hair Out of Place—The

Illusion of Perfection

Strong women don't have "attitudes," we have standards. –Marilyn Monroe

What is one thing that women and leaders have in common? Both have a standard of infallible perfection placed upon them, regardless of who they are, what they do, and who else has ever made a mistake. Both women, leaders, and especially women who lead, are forced to be nothing less than perfect, lest they are looked upon as incompetent. This illusion of perfection equaling good leadership is nothing more than a misconception.

You do not have to be perfect to be a good leader. And wild women are far from perfect, which is something we embrace—our unique flaws and strengths alike make us who we are. In a society that prizes perfection, it can be challenging to assert yourself as a leader when you have expectations and stereotypes running against you. But in this chapter, you will learn to not only embrace your imperfections, but to challenge those who force perfection upon you as well.

Perfectionism and Women: A Subtle Expectation

You are not likely to hear someone state, "I expect women to be perfect," yet it is a domineering shadow looming over all women. In relationships, women are expected to be almost robotic in how flawless they are; in workplaces, one mistake can jeopardize your whole reputation. Men, however, do not find that same treatment very often, routinely getting three, four, five, or more mistakes before anyone bats an eye.

Understanding the harsh implications of perfectionism that women face day in and day out is the key to unlocking a future where we wild women are truly free. A mistake here or there should not make us look *un*credible, we should be viewed as *in*credible! Let's dive into how women and the expectation of perfectionism impact us.

Fashion and Beauty Expectations

Fashion and beauty are two industries where you should be able to be yourself, using the tools and skills involved to express who you are and who you are growing into. Unfortunately, people perceive fashion and beauty as something to use to attain perfection. Women push that onto themselves, while men push it onto women.

One prominent example of this is the anti-aging industry. The anti-aging industry is less about helping women feel good about themselves and more about making us aesthetically appealing to others, which is not what it should be all about. Aging is a gift; not everyone is fortunate enough to reach old age. And yet, people use anti-aging to hide that gift and make women feel bad about the natural progression of their bodies.

Fashion does the same. Every day, you see people online say that someone who weighs X number of pounds should not wear an article of clothing. Wild women who dress freely and vibrantly are told to tone it down for the workplace. And forget about extreme makeup that shows off your artistic talents—that's "too much."

All of this culminates in telling women that they have to be perfect according to a standard that we did not even set. We have to look young, but not too young. We have to wear makeup, but only if it is invisible. Expressing yourself as a woman is "unprofessional" according to these standards.

This is just a single facet of how society, both in and outside of the workplace, expects women to look and behave perfectly. Women who do not conform to these standards are seen as bad leaders *and* bad followers, unprofessional, sloppy, try-hards, or anything else under the rainbow. In reality, we women who do not conform are the wild women who exist in the in-between—and we make some of the best leaders.

One Strike and You Are Out!

There is also a common tendency for businesses, individuals, partners, and more to have a one-strike system when it comes to women. For a man, making a mistake is just a normal Tuesday; it is something that happens, we all get over it, and then we go about our lives. But for a woman, one mistake can undermine her credibility, lose her position, and otherwise tarnish what she has worked so hard for. But why is that?

There are conflicting opinions on this, but from first-hand experience, interviews, and research, I think I can isolate exactly why society is far more lenient with men who make mistakes than women. Men are allowed to make mistakes because our society encourages men to take risks and be domineering. On the other hand, women are thought of as submissive and agreeable.

Therefore, when a woman makes a mistake, it is perceived to be an inherent flaw of her character. For a man, it is just nature—mistakes are natural. This means that, because women made a mistake, they are thought of as disagreeable, unruly, uncareful, and more, otherwise destroying any credibility they had.

You and I can both see how unfair this is. While it might be near-impossible to correct this societal bias on your own, you can stop this attitude of perfection from influencing your ability to be a confident and wild woman. This can be accomplished through refusing to let a mistake ruin your day, or even put a dent in your confidence. Embrace your mistakes as a learning experience.

Moreover, the skills that you will pick up throughout the course of this book will help you overcome both the likelihood of making mistakes as well as the suppression of who you are. But for now, let's take a look at some dynamic women who, while imperfect, are legendary leaders.

Imperfect Women Who Are Legendary Leaders

Throughout history, there have been countless women who are imperfect, but many of them found notoriety as leaders in one way or another. Just a few of those women include

- **Maya Angelou:** Ms. Angelou was one of the most famous poets in history. She stated that she experienced a constant fear of not being good enough—that one poem would show her as a fraud. That never happened; eventually, she embraced her wild and became a beacon of justice and equality, fighting for what was right through her passion and imperfections.

- **Ruth Bader Ginsburg:** While imperfect and facing many obstacles, Ginsburg was a late Supreme Court Justice who pioneered significant movements toward gender equality in the United States.

- **Malala Yousafzai:** A wild woman if I've ever seen one, Malala managed to survive an assassination attempt on her road to seeking education as a woman in a heavily patriarchal society. Now, she is an inspirational and radiant figure for girls everywhere!

- **Serena Williams:** A tennis legend, Serena is known for her determination and strength, both on and off the court, challenging stereotypes and breaking barriers. She has never let a stereotype or struggle stop her in the face of what she wants to achieve!

- **Frida Kahlo:** A celebrated painter—and no painter is perfect—Kahlo allowed her art to reflect her imperfections in a profound way, which is part of the reason why she is so famous for her work to this day.

As you can see, a lot of expectations regarding perfection are forced onto women. Meanwhile, some of the best leaders are the ones who make mistakes and embrace them as a part of the process!

Perfectionism and Leadership

Perfectionism is something that leaders of all genders face, often due to the fact that people think leaders have to be perfect. This section explores the link between perfectionism and leadership, ultimately proving that leaders can still make mistakes and be more powerful than their "perfect" counterparts.

Why Perfectionists Make Bad Leaders

Being a leader is not all about being perfect. Many people believe that perfectionists—those obsessed with doing everything perfectly all of the time—would make the best leaders, but they do not! It's actually the people who are willing to take risks, make mistakes, and learn from them who we can see and behold as some of the best leaders. This goes for both men and women.

But why exactly do perfectionists make such poor leaders? There are several reasons for this. For one, perfectionists make poor leaders because they allow their fear of failure to drive their every move. There is a difference between cautious and perfectionist, and those who are unwilling to take calculated risks in order to achieve a goal certainly fall into the latter category.

In addition, perfectionists tend to take on more than they can handle because they do not feel like anyone can live up to their standards but themselves. This can lead to micromanaging or otherwise making team members feel pressured or unwanted, tearing apart the functions of a team from the inside out. In contrast, a manager who balances wild with caution typically empowers their team to try things out, make mistakes, and pick themselves back up.

Perfectionists also struggle to adapt to changes and burn themselves out quickly. This means that they are not dependable when someone flexible is needed and that their effort and abilities will fizzle out from how hard they work themselves. Moreover, perfectionist leaders are more likely to have outbursts and mistreat their staff.

In all, perfectionists make poor leaders because they do not adapt or grow. There's no room for ideas to be shared and risks to be taken under the leadership of a perfectionist. And while this may seem like a safe route to go, it is also the route that keeps a company or team from flourishing.

How Scuffs Make You Shine

A perfect leader is one who is imperfect. The scuffs that you have, be it a character flaw, a mentality or bias, or just a lack of skill in certain areas actually make you a more powerful leader in many ways. People who embrace their imperfections are more willing and able to ask for help, calling in other opinions and the skills of others to make *everyone* happy rather than just themselves.

Also, leaders who embrace imperfection have a growth mindset and an openness to learning. Someone who is a perfectionist thinks that they have the best ways down already; someone who embraces their scuffs is willing to learn from others, bettering themselves in the process. This means that all members of the team get the opportunity to feel valued and heard.

Leaders who recognize their shortcomings also contribute to environments that pride themselves on innovation, growth, improvement, trust, and resilience. In all of my years, the most fortuitous places I've worked have been places where the leaders allowed everyone's opinion to count equally, where if a challenge came up, we all overcame it. This is exactly what happens in an environment where someone with self-awareness is leading.

That said, I strongly believe that women are more able to recognize their mistakes, delegate tasks effectively, and show empathy in the workplace. Studies verify this train of thought, which is why I feel confident in stating that wild women are the best leaders, especially if they are flawed (Agaragimova, 2022).

Understanding Good Leadership

In Chapter 1, we talked about some elements that are intrinsically linked to successful leadership. Some of those factors included emotional intelligence, empathy, and creativity. Nobody is perfect, but women are better able to embrace that perfection because, as mentioned in the last chapter, women are more in tune with these factors that add up to a good leader.

Of course, that's not to say that all men are bad leaders. Rather, the point of this is to say that even if a woman makes a mistake or has a flaw, something typically frowned upon due to less lenience, it does not mean that she's a bad leader. In fact, a flawed woman makes a better leader due to a higher aptitude for strong leadership traits mentioned in the last section and in Chapter 1.

Men vs. Women: Mistake Showdown

Some people will argue that companies are harsher on women because they tend to make more mistakes, but that truly is not the case. Depending on the research that you look at, you can find that men often make more mistakes that can impact leadership than women do, or that the two are equal. Let's look at some numbers:

- When considering empathy, one study of over 300,000 people—spanning more than 50 countries—indicated that women are significantly more empathetic than men (*Females on Average Perform Better*, 2022). This suggests that women are less likely to make empathy-related errors in the workplace.

- One study showed that women are 6.5% more likely to listen to, retain, *and* consider information spoken to them, implying that women may make fewer communication-related errors (Zenger, n.d.).

- Women are statistically more likely to apologize for wrongdoings than men, indicating that women may have a higher aptitude for overcoming mistakes and finding solutions rather than deflecting blame (Morin, 2019).

Now, this is not about debating if men or women are better—that's not how it works. Rather, these studies show that *both* men and women make mistakes and that women excel in handling those mistakes in certain ways (while men probably excel at other methods of handling them). All this shows is that men *and* women can both make mistakes and still competently hold skills that make them good leaders.

Again, it is not about who quantifiably makes mistakes. But from this, we can see that women may have the upper hand when it comes to communication and empathetic problem-solving, which means that even if women make mistakes, we have profoundly notable ways to fix them. Therefore, there is no reason to exclude or deny the credibility of a woman on the basis of one—or a few—mistakes. And while you already knew this, having the proof in front of you can sure boost your confidence!

Mistakes are not what makes a leader bad; in fact, mistakes can make a leader age like fine wine. Now that you understand how scuffs can make your strengths shine, you do not have to worry about being perfect as a leader—just about doing your best and being yourself.

Wild Woman Rituals

Keeping up with being a wild woman is hard, which is why I've devised some wild woman rituals to help you embrace and practice your wildness. In Chapters 2 through 9, you'll find that these activities are relevant to the chapter itself, helping you either practice your skills or find your confidence when it comes to shouting passion, flavor, and drive from the rooftops. Let's see what the wild woman's rituals for this chapter are!

The Wild Affirmations

An affirmation is a statement that you repeat to yourself over and over, eventually giving you confidence and reassurance that that statement is true. There are a lot of people who believe that affirmations do not work, but I can tell you from first-hand experience that they do. If you tell yourself something enough times, then eventually you *will* believe it, good or bad. Might as well make it good!

Below are 10 wild woman affirmations that you can use for your own practice. Every day, find three different times to repeat the affirmations that resonate the most with you. This can be aloud while looking into a mirror, in your head, or even by writing them down:

1. I embrace my wild spirit and allow it to guide me toward my truest self.

2. My confidence grows as I connect with the untamed power within me.

3. I am a force of nature, unapologetically bold and fiercely authentic.

4. I trust the wisdom of my intuition, letting it lead me on my unique journey.

5. I celebrate my flaws as the beautiful marks of a life fully lived.

6. My strength comes from within, and I trust in my ability to overcome any challenge.

7. I release the need for perfection and revel in the beauty of my imperfections.

8. Every step I take is a dance with my own rhythm, a celebration of my individuality.

9. I am a wild woman, free to express myself authentically and without inhibition.

10. In the wildness of my soul, I discover the limitless reservoir of confidence that propels me forward with grace and power.

In addition, here is some space to create five more affirmations of your very own:

1.

2.

3.

4.

5.

The Resilience Worksheet

Everybody makes mistakes, but some of us take those mistakes harder than others do. In this worksheet, you will be invited to explore your mistakes and realize that you are not defined by them.

Date: _____

What is a recent mistake that you've made—one that you cannot stop thinking about?

_____
_____
_____
_____
_____
_____

What were the circumstances of the mistake? When, where, why, and so on?

_____

_____
_____
_____
_____
_____
_____
_____
_____

What impact did the mistake have?

_____
_____
_____
_____
_____
_____
_____
_____

How do _you_ feel about the mistake?

_____
_____
_____
_____
_____
_____
_____

Do you truly feel as though the mistake was your fault?
[YES/NO]

**If you had to sum up your feelings about the mistake in one
sentence, what would you say?**

_____

_____

_____

_____

_____

_____

Is that thought helpful? [YES/NO]

Does it contribute to your life in a positive way? [YES/NO]

With that in mind, what is a more positive and helpful way to reframe your one sentence?

_____

_____

_____

_____

_____

_____

_____

When it comes to being a wild woman, you do not have to be perfect—in fact, in order to be a wild woman, you have to embrace those imperfections like a badge of honor. Being imperfect does not mean that you are a bad leader, either. Some of the best leaders, as a matter of fact, are the ones who can make a mistake and curtly acknowledge it, learning and growing from it as a result.

With that said, you do not have to be a perfect, Barbie-esque superhero to make a compassionate leader who embraces being wild. You just need a few skills to help let that wildness within you shine, and it all starts with communication. In the next chapter, I'm going to show you exactly how you can communicate as a leader—without scaring off the villagers of your audience!

Chapter 3:

The Banshee's Wail–Vocal,

Powerful Communication

Women have to be active listeners and interrupters. But when you interrupt, you have to know what you're talking about. –Madeleine Albright

One of the most valuable skills for any leader is communication; without proper communication, nothing gets done or resolved. For women, however, there are frequently unique communication struggles that we have to overcome in order for our voices to be heard. That's what this chapter is all about—balancing obstacle dodging alongside fierce communication that will not scare off the villagers!

Finding Your Voice

Not all leaders are leaders in the workplace. You can lead at school, home, or anywhere else. However, in order to lead, you need to be able to find your voice. Your voice is what makes your communication your own. It involves how you communicate, why you communicate, and the methods that you use to express what you have to say. For many women, finding a voice can be hard because we are often shut down.

Women Often Get Shut Down

What do I mean when I say that women get shut down? Well, think about it. Has anyone ever told you that you are being too loud, long-winded, need to get to the point, or anything similar? Has anyone ever made you feel like you could not speak or that your ideas are not important? If that or anything similar has happened, then I can tell you now that you've been shut down!

There are actually studies that show how men interrupting and shutting down women is a common phenomenon (Coker, 2022). In other words, it is not just you; all women have some story of men interrupting them or shutting them down. Usually, this either stems from an inflated ego or a sense of needing to assert dominance, but some men do not even know that they are interrupting you.

The impact of being shut down is, I believe, far more important than the act of being shut down. In other words, it is more important for us to focus on the impact that it has had on you than it is for us to focus on *why* you've been shut down. Some of the common impacts of being shut down can include

- **Low self-esteem:** When someone is constantly interrupted, spoken over, shot down, or discouraged in communication, it can lead to marked impacts on self-esteem. Many women suffer from low self-confidence due to being consistently told that their voice does not matter.

- **Communication deficiencies:** When someone is spoken over, especially in the context of decision-making in leadership, there are communication deficiencies. Not only do you not know how to speak and communicate because you never get to practice, but others do not understand your perspective.

- **Misunderstandings:** Being shut down also means that all parties involved are going to fundamentally misunderstand one another. You cannot understand someone whose opinion you do not know, much like you also cannot understand an opinion that does not consider all points of view.

- **Weak relationships:** Chances are, your relationship with someone who cannot communicate without shutting you down is going to be very weak. This can be particularly troubling in the context of a relationship.

That said, it is important to find ways to overcome being shut down, as well as the impacts that being shut down can have. One of the best ways that you can do this is through finding your voice.

How to Find Your Voice

In order to overcome the influences of being shut down, the first thing that you need to do is find a voice—your voice. If you do not already have a bit of an understanding of what your voice entails, then you might have trouble with this. Do not worry—I'm here to help!

Step 1: Understand Your Values

The first step involved in finding your voice is understanding your values. When you communicate, you have a value in mind that you are either trying to express or striving to align with. Leaders always have something they value, whether it is money, cohesion, recognition, or happiness.

But how do you discover your values? In order to find what is meaningful to you and what drives your voice, think about your role as a leader. Are you leading a company or a family? Something in between? Think about what you want to accomplish by leading in that particular context. Then, consider what it is that you want the people you are leading to walk away from after the conversation.

Understanding your values might be a challenge at first. Ask yourself what the most important takeaway of your speech would be. Try to truly encapsulate that in one sentence, and you have your values—at least for the context of a particular conversation. Part of having a voice of your own means distinctly referring back to those values throughout, as your values become your voice in a sense.

Step 2: Be Confident

Then, it is important that you speak confidently. This can be another challenging aspect of finding your voice as a woman, especially because many women are told to push their voices down. Being confident as a wild woman means that you should speak your mind—which does not mean being disrespectful, as many people wrongly assume.

In order to confidently speak your mind, you have to talk like you own the room. This means that you should work to eliminate filler words like "um" and "uh" from your vocabulary. It also means discerning what confidence is and is not (i.e., confidence in speaking is *not* talking over others). As you speak, you are going to need to sound like you know what you are talking about, which helps if you really do.

Speak with conviction, letting your opinions be your own. Try not to say "I think..." too much, and instead, get to the point more concisely. For example, why would you say, "I think we should start an email newsletter to improve engagement," when "an email newsletter would improve our engagement tenfold" is shorter and sounds far more assured? Confidence also comes with knowing your stuff, so make sure you can back your ideas up!

Step 3: Slow Down

A lot of women speak very rapidly due to the fact that if they do not, they know they'll get cut off. Rather than speaking rapidly to accommodate the rude behavior of others, speak confidently and slowly. At the end of the chapter, there are ways that you can steer the conversation back to yourself if someone interrupts you; for now, let's focus on this skill.

Slowing down means not rushing over your words and tripping up your sentences. Each sentence and even each word should be calculated, adding something to your communication. Slowing down results in more concise, filler-free dialogue, and it also shows others that they have to wait for you to finish. Coupled with refusing to let someone interrupt you, your voice will unfold naturally.

Step 4: Know When to Stop

At the same time, refusing to let someone interrupt you assumes that they want to hear what you have to say in the first place. Some people simply do not care about opinions other than their own, and you cannot make them. If someone refuses to let you have a turn when conversing, simply state, "Since I am not being given the courtesy of uninterrupted time to speak, I will have to end this conversation."

Assertiveness 101

Developing a sense of assertiveness can be challenging when people are constantly opposing your authority, competence, and more. At the same time, assertiveness is a vital skill for confident, wild women who do not let others step all over them, especially in conversation. The good news is that being assertive is as simple as picking up a few specific communication skills.

For example, you need to make eye contact. Eye contact on its own is already more assertive than most women regularly engage in when communicating. It says "I mean business" to anyone you are talking to. Even if you look at their forehead, nose, between their eyes, or another area around the eyes, it will have the same commandeering nature as staring them right in the pupils.

Furthermore, assertively wild women know when to say "no." If someone is making you uncomfortable, asking you to take on more than your fair share, or otherwise giving you a reason to say "no," then say it! You do not have to defend your "no," and if you do not offer up an explanation, you seem more assertive. For instance, "Sorry, I cannot stay late because I have a date" is far less assertive than "No, I am unable to stay late tonight."

It can also be helpful to practice what it is that you want to say ahead of time. Especially when you start communicating with your wild side leading you, it can be hard to come up with your dialogue on the fly. Practicing ahead, especially for important conversations or presentations, can make others view you as more assertive.

Women and Imposter Syndrome

Fifty-three percent of women suffer from imposter syndrome or will experience it at some point in their lives; 54% of men *never* experience it, and 63% of the men who do only experience imposter syndrome at work (*Women More Likely to Suffer from Imposter Syndrome*, 2023). We can thus say that imposter syndrome is a big deal for us women.

Imposter syndrome is a major roadblock in finding your voice as a wild woman. Imposter syndrome refers to the inability to accept that your status, recognition, or achievements are legitimate. For example, many women with imposter syndrome believe that their accomplishments are due to the fact that they have fooled or tricked someone into believing that they are capable.

Overcoming imposter syndrome is a major step forward in finding your voice and embracing the fact that the wild parts of you are an accomplishment and beacon of achievement, as well as realizing that you are not an imposter. Some ways that you can fight off the wicked force of imposter syndrome include

- **Rejecting perfectionism:** Many women with imposter syndrome suffer because they believe that if their efforts are imperfect, then they should not be recognized. For instance, believing that you should not have gotten a promotion due to a mistake you made is imposter syndrome-related perfectionism.

- **Be kind to yourself:** You have no reason to assume that you are an imposter, nor to beat yourself up for others recognizing the good in you. When you have a thought that screams that you are not smart, funny, knowledgeable, wise, or experienced enough, conquer that thought with some affirmations and confidence—even if you have to fake it 'til you make it!

- **Measure and celebrate success:** To you, it might seem like you have not accomplished much. If you measure and celebrate those successes, however, you'll soon realize that you've done way more than you believe.

- **"Imposter" is a skill:** Even if you cannot force yourself to believe that you are not an imposter, realize that being an imposter is actually a skill. If you can successfully seem capable across anything you do, then you are not only capable at everything you do, but you are capable of looking like a legendary wild woman while doing so.

Overall, finding your voice serves as a crucial element in allowing your values, considerations, and opinions to take hold in a leadership setting. Wild women need to find alignment with this voice to let their skills and talents be recognized unilaterally.

Fierce and Effective Communication

Outside of finding your voice, there are still a few different communication considerations that you should take to heart. These communication techniques specifically will help you bring your wild to the conversation without freaking those around you out—after all, beholding a wild woman is no easy task!

Be Descriptive

As you speak, you need to be descriptive. Do not just say, "It is important that customers engage with our new content." Say what you *mean*; say, "It is crucial that customers are energetic and thrilled by our new content. It should leave an impression on their minds that they cannot shake." You have to drive home exactly what you want using all five senses to describe things.

Use Your Body

In addition, you should use your whole body to communicate. From facial expressions to hand gestures and all of the body language in between, it is important that you talk the talk and walk the walk. That means that your body language has to match the words you are saying; if you state that your company needs to raise excitement, so should your body language. It's vital that you use your body!

This means that you should engage your face with what you are saying. Let your eyebrows raise to indicate shock or surprise, and smile if you are happy. Similarly, a stern talk should not have accompanying facial expressions of glee. Stand up tall and confidently, and use your hands to gesture as you talk. A confident speaker is one who uses all of their resources, and the subtle cues of your body certainly amplify your message.

Bring the Energy

You have to bring energy to the conversation. Wild women are brimming with it, so make sure that your words, expressions, and engagement with your audience—whether it is one person or 500—shows energy. You cannot convey a topic to a yawning, bored audience, so do not be afraid to show them that you are truly excited about what you have to share!

Be a Good Listener

Finally, and most importantly, when it comes to not scaring people off, you have to be a good listener. Invite people to speak and share their opinions, and actively listen to those opinions as well. Make sure that people feel comfortable sharing ideas with you by not interrupting or shutting others down, and encourage people to toss brainstorming out there even if it is not "useful." Moreover, ensure that everyone feels heard and like their perspective matters.

At the end of the day, communication is not just a skill—it is an art. And by practicing and learning more and more about communicating, you can set your best foot forward as a wild woman known for her passionate communication, empathetic listening, and advantageous ideas that shoot for the stars (and make it there, too).

Wild Woman Rituals

Welcome back to your wild woman rituals! These activities center themselves around communication, helping you overcome challenges and get yourself into the habit of working with some of the best practices for communication. Take a look at what you have to work with today!

Dialogue for Being Spoken Over

Alright, so you've got someone who thinks they can talk over you on your hands. Sometimes, you might not know what to say, which is why I've devised this dialogue checklist that you can use if someone is trying to talk over you, each offering a unique tone or perspective.

- "I appreciate your input, and I'll let you know when I'm finished speaking."

- "I have not finished my point yet; please allow me to complete it."

- "I value your perspective, but I would like the opportunity to express my thoughts without interruption."

- "Let's make sure we are giving each other space to speak. I'll finish, and then I'm eager to hear your thoughts."

- "As I was saying..."

- "To go back to my earlier point..."

- Maintain eye contact and a firm posture to signal that you are not finished speaking.

- Raise a hand slightly to indicate that you'd like to continue.

- "I find it challenging to convey my thoughts when interrupted. Can we ensure we give each other time to speak?"

- "Let's create an environment where everyone has an opportunity to express their ideas without interruptions."

- "I must be really interesting today; I keep getting interrupted!"

- "I feel like I'm on a talk show with all these interruptions. Can I finish my monologue?"

- "I'd like to hear your thoughts but let me finish first. Then, I'm all ears for your perspective."

- "After I'm done, I'd love to hear your insights on this."

- "To ensure we are all on the same page, let's make sure we give everyone a chance to share their thoughts."

- "Our discussion will be more productive if we each have a chance to express our viewpoints without interruptions."

- "I understand this is an engaging conversation, but I'd appreciate a moment to complete my thoughts."

- "I value your input, and I'm looking forward to hearing it. Let me finish, and then it is all yours."

- "I need to finish my point, so please let me speak without interruptions."

- "I'll make sure to give you the same courtesy when you are speaking, so let's ensure we both have uninterrupted time."

The "I" Statements Guide

An "I" statement is one that begins with the word "I" and conveys your feelings about a topic or event. They can often be preferable in back-and-forth dialogue, as "I" statements do not have an accusatory tone and reframe things in a light where we take responsibility for ourselves. You should be using these types of statements as a leader.

Below, use the table to practice reframing accusatory, unfair, or inappropriate statements into respectful yet honest "I" statements. The first one is filled out for you.

Original statement	"I" statement
You never let me finish what I'm trying to say!	I am having a hard time expressing what I need to say due to being interrupted; please let me finish my point, and then I will listen to what you have to say.
Maybe if you did not... this would not keep happening.	
You were wrong, and that's why we are in this situation.	
Your idea is not going to work because...	
Are you even qualified to make that judgment?	

My Communication Style: Journaling

Now, it is time to journal a bit about your communication style. Write down your responses to the next two prompts to see how you can work toward improving your communication style!

My biggest flaw when communicating as a leader is

_____
_____
_____
_____
_____
_____
_____
_____

I can improve that flaw by

_____
_____
_____
_____
_____
_____
_____
_____

In all, it is vital to understand how to communicate as a wild woman. Often, no one teaches us how to communicate; instead, they try to shut us down entirely. But with the right communication skills, you can communicate your passion and ambitions wholeheartedly, and be a rockstar while doing so. Next up, we are going to take a look at risk-taking—every wild woman's favorite task.

Chapter 4:

Wild, Not Reckless—The Boldness

of Calculated Risks

Only those who will risk going too far can possibly find out how far one can go. –T. S. Eliot

As a leader, whether that be the leader of a company or a family, taking risks is important. Risks are how we develop and grow, achieving more in life. But at the same time, risks are risky. As a wild woman, it is important that you can walk the razor's edge of risk-taking, making bold and daring yet intellectual decisions in the risk-taking game. This chapter serves as your guide for doing just that.

Taking Risks With Skill

Taking risks is a skill in and of itself. Being a wild woman does not mean being a reckless one, and being a boss-like leader does not mean playing it totally safe. In this section, you are going to unlock the secrets to skillful risk-taking for wild women who never back down and never let the ship sink (while they are still standing on it, at least).

Understanding Risk Taking

What does it mean to take a risk? If you answered with something like "taking a risk means to give something a chance, even if you do not know whether it will work out," then you are exactly right! A key element of taking a risk is charging forward, even when there is an air of uncertainty surrounding your decisions. Risk-taking is calculated; being reckless is not taking a risk because recklessness is an entirely different affair altogether.

There are many benefits to taking risks, especially for wild women. In fact, wild women are aligned with risk-taking specifically because of our unstoppable, brave nature. By taking risks, you

- gain access to unexpected or unforeseen opportunities. This can take your company, your family, or yourself to unexpected heights of success.

- foster resilience and an adaptation to change, ultimately making you and yours stronger and more resistant in the face of challenge.

- build up your credibility each and every time a risk lands successfully. And with the right confidence and communication skills, a failed risk will not hurt you.

- learn more about the industry, field, or dynamics in which you engage, granting you a fuller understanding of the world around you.

And much more. Beyond that, understanding skillful risk-taking can reduce the number of people who look down on you for mistakes— something that does, unfortunately, occur disproportionately to women, as discussed in Chapter 2.

Risk vs. Reckless

Many people, even wild women, wrongly assume that recklessness and risk-taking are one and the same when, in reality, that could not be further from the truth! While related, the concepts have certain distinctions that are crucial when deciding whether to take a risk, action, or step forward.

Specifically, risk-taking involves making decisions or engaging in activities where there is a chance of gaining a positive outcome, but there is also a potential for negative consequences. Investments are a common form of risk, whether that's a stock investment or an investment in your own side hustle. Some defining characteristics of risk-taking include

- **Calculative:** A good risk is one that is calculative, meaning that you have to weigh the benefits and drawbacks before you make a decision—otherwise, your decision is reckless and uninformed.

- **Goal-oriented:** Risks are usually made with a goal in mind. Those who take risks do so in order to potentially achieve a certain outcome.

- **Measured:** Those who embark upon a risk take measured and intentional steps to get there, rather than going all in with no strategy.

On the other hand, you have recklessness. Recklessness specifically refers to a lack of regard for potential consequences that can arise from one's actions. Even if you think you've considered everything, you still need proper, careful consideration to move from reckless to risk. Some key features of reckless behavior include

- **Impulsive:** Everyone has impulses, but acting on them can be quite reckless due to the lack of careful planning and consideration of outcomes.

- **Short-term focus:** Many reckless decisions are made with consideration only for the short term. This can often bring about long-term consequences, even if the reckless behavior works out for now.

- **Lack of consideration:** Reckless individuals may not fully appreciate the potential dangers or negative consequences associated with their actions. They act without due consideration for the impact on themselves or others.

With that being said, you can master the art of being a wild woman without having to be a reckless, inconsiderate one. The two are not one and the same. Managing risks intelligently is as simple as four easy skills!

Skill 1: Considering All Options

In order to truly take risks as a magnificent, wild woman who is not reckless, one of the first skills that you need is the skill to consider all of your available options before you engage with a risk. This starts with the process of clearly defining a goal. For example, let's say that you are at work and brainstorming ideas to increase customer engagement. Your goal, then, is to boost customer engagement, and you should probably outline specifically what "boosting" means to you.

Then, you have to consider your options. You have a team with you and you are pitching ideas. One person suggests an email campaign, which you've done in the past. It does boost engagement, but only marginally. Someone else suggests a campaign that you have not tried, and while it does take financial investment, other companies who have done it have had major success.

You can play it safe, or you can consider the riskier—and potentially more rewarding—option. Some choices that you have for truly weighing your options include

- Gathering information about each alternative. Depending on the scenario, you will need to gather information. With our example in mind, you might think about past success rates, costs, and so on.

- Assessing the risks against the benefits. Think about what the worst and best-case scenarios are for your options, and determine whether the risks of each option outweigh the realistic best-case scenario.

- Analyzing the probability. It's good to consider the most likely outcome of each situation, rather than solely thinking about the ideal outcome.

After considering your options, you need to employ Skill 2.

Skill 2: The Pros and Cons

Weighing the pros and cons of all of your options is a great skill to have, especially when it comes to risk-taking. If you are not already aware, the pros of a scenario are potential benefits, while the cons are drawbacks. In order to consider the pros and cons of a situation carefully, you need to think about a few different things.

For example, it is always good to consider the resources necessary for a goal or risk to be set in motion. And resources are not just financial. Of course, preparing for the financial side of things is important, especially for work, but you also have to take into consideration other resources. Time, space, skill, and other resources are all spent when you take a risk. Pros and cons can help you understand the resource expenditure of an option.

You also have to consider the possibility of each option. It might, by all technicality, be possible to run the second suggested campaign, but how possible is it for *you* to run it? If you are strapped for resources and time, then that might not be an option. This pairs with considering the likelihood of a positive outcome. Many risks have at least some possibility of failure—after all, they are called risks—but something that would take a miracle to come true might be more reckless than risk.

There are many ways to weigh pros and cons, such as

- Email campaign

    o Pro: Free, easy, and accessible

    o Con: Low likelihood of complete success

- Risky campaign

    o Pro: High likelihood of significant success

    o Con: Financially risky

This is when it can be helpful to also take the time to predict outcomes.

Skill 3: Predicting Outcomes

Predicting outcomes when taking a risk involves a combination of careful analysis, informed decision-making, and an understanding of the factors involved. It might seem a bit restrictive compared to completely impulsive decision-making, but all smart, wild women know when to be diplomatic. That said, some strategies you can use for predicting the outcome of situations before taking a risk include

- **Research:** When you are considering a risk, try to do some research and find out as much as you can about potential outcomes. This might be historical trends, learning from the experiences of others, or otherwise seeing what the outcomes could be based on evidence.

- **Assess the risk:** Consider the benefits, drawbacks, and probability to get a well-rounded view of the potential outcomes that may arise from a particular risk.

- **Consider the alternatives:** It can be helpful to think about what you would do instead if the first choice/biggest risk is not an option. This is a simple thought process that avoids bias and allows you to think about other outcomes for a more intelligent risk evaluation.

- **Risk tolerance:** Your risk tolerance describes how much uncertainty and/or potential loss you are willing to tolerate in exchange for the potential benefits of the risk. Wild women are known for their fierce risk tolerance, so be sure to consider whether those around you have lower risk tolerance.

- **Scenario planning:** It can be helpful to consider the alternatives by devising a contingency plan for the various scenarios that may unfold.

Skill 4: Asking for (and Accepting) Feedback

Finally, you should ask for and accept the feedback of others—before, during, and after taking a risk. Even though wild women are very good at considering the interlocking circumstances of a situation, it can be helpful to gain the opinions and expertise of those around you. By asking for and accepting feedback with an open mind, you can not only improve your ability to take risks in the future, but you can also assert yourself as an open, honest, compassionate, and loyal leader.

In all, these four skills will set you up for abundant success when it comes to taking risks that avoid recklessness. Some of the best brainstorming sessions can come from that unfettered wildness that leads to impulsive, chaotic decisions, but earnestly considering risks is vital for profound outcomes.

The Ancient Art of Not Falling Flat on Your Face

Nothing is worse than taking calculated steps toward a goal, only for everything to come crashing down around you, making you look like a fool in the process. In earlier chapters, I mentioned the forces that work against you when it comes to being a wild woman in leadership positions. And while those forces are not your fault, nor should you have to conform to them, it can make things far easier if you know how to avoid falling flat on your face. Let's see what it takes.

Common Risk-Taking Mistakes (and How to Avoid Them)

Taking a risk often involves a unique blend of innovation, experience, and willingness to mess up. At the same time, being a wild woman means that messing up might not be on your agenda—which is totally fine. In order to mitigate this concern, it is important to understand common mistakes that are made when taking risks and what you can do to avoid them.

For one, many people dive into risks without properly analyzing them. It can be great to have a strong foundational understanding of the benefits associated with a risk, but if you do not take the time to analyze outcomes, expenditures, benefits, drawbacks, and more, you may just fall flat on your face while taking a risk. Fortunately, this is simply avoided by using the analysis strategies provided to you earlier in the chapter. While it may seem boring or time-consuming to analyze a risk, it is better to be bored now than to be embarrassed down the road.

Another mistake that people often make when it comes to taking a risk is forgetting or refusing to manage that risk continuously. Returning to our previous example, you might have opted to go with the riskier campaign for higher customer involvement—that's awesome! As a result, sales and interactions skyrocketed. At the same time—you got very comfortable with that risk and its initial success. This means that you are no longer managing the risk, and to your surprise, it actually backfires with engagement dropping lower than ever before.

This is just one instance of how poor risk management and continuous assessment can jeopardize your success and integrity. Rather than falling victim to this simple risk management mistake, you can mitigate it by keeping tabs on your risks regularly. You do not have to watch them like a hawk—after all, we wild women have other things to do—but regularly returning to consider how a risk is panning out can help you manage that risk continuously—achieving more success in the process.

The third biggest mistake that people make when it comes to risk-taking is ignoring opportunities. This is especially common in women who are afraid to slip up due to a risk; however, branching out and considering all available opportunities will not only help you find new risks to take, but it will also ensure that the risks you do take are the best of all options.

Managing Negative Outcomes and Damage Control

We may be wild, but we are not perfect. Embracing that imperfection also involves understanding that our outcomes can have negative consequences. As a result, it is good to know how you can manage negative outcomes and run damage control on failed risks. Situationally, this will depend, as a mother managing a household will have different strategies than a CEO, but overall, there are a few tricks you can employ in just five steps:

1. **Understand why the risk failed:** When a risk has had a negative outcome, the best thing that you can do is take a step back and consider why the risk failed. Sometimes, the culprit will be obvious; other times, you are going to have to do some analysis. Understanding why your risk failed will massively improve risk taking moving forward.

2. **Consider the damages:** After understanding the "why," consider the "how." How did the risk fail, and what was the impact that it had? Identifying the damages, if any, is important to understanding what you have to fix and how to prevent such damages moving forward.

3. **Cut some losses:** After a risk, some things are not able to be salvaged. Determine what you can save, and let go of what you cannot. Trying to cling to and resolve losses can be a risk in and of itself—one that expends more resources in the clean-up of the original risk!

4. **Take accountability:** It can be tempting to try and point fingers at others. After all, many women face unique pressure as leaders. Even still, you should be sure to own up for the mistakes that you have made, as in the long run, this does show that you are a go-getter *and* willing to take responsibility.

5. **Move forward gracefully:** Move forward, having learned from your mistakes and take risks that are bigger and better than ever.

How to Learn From Mistakes

Learning from mistakes might be a tough pill to swallow; it means admitting that you have done something wrong, which can be a big deal for many! But it is important to learn from mistakes because they can serve as our biggest teachers. Learning from mistakes shows you how to improve your goals, actions, and steps moving forward. In order to learn from mistakes, all you have to do is consider why the mistake was a mistake in the first place. Then, you have the ability to avoid making the mistake again.

In all, falling on your face can be embarrassing, but it is a chance to show how wild you are by dusting yourself off with a smile. Everyone makes mistakes, and wild women are particularly powerful at shaking them off and making a comeback.

Wild Woman Rituals

The wild woman rituals of this chapter are aimed at helping you improve your ability to take and manage risks responsibly, while still maintaining that wildness you so love. That way, when the time comes to exercise your risk-taking muscles, you will know just how to do so with tact, grace, and, of course, the howl of the wild.

Risk Tolerance Development

No matter how wild you are, taking a risk for the first time of your own accord can be hard—especially because we live in a society where risky women are called irresponsible. Spoiler alert: We are not! We just know how to play our cards perfectly, and through developing a tolerance to risk, so can you.

Below is a risk tolerance worksheet-based challenge. Fill it out and engage with the prompts, even copying it down to use a few times over. As you do, you will slowly become more tolerant of taking risks!

Name three risks that you want to take this week:

1. _____

2. _____

3. _____

Which of those risks seems the most daunting and why?

_____
_____
_____
_____
_____
_____
_____
_____
_____

What do you think the outcome of that risk would be? How would you feel after completing it?

_____
_____
_____
_____
_____
_____
_____
_____
_____

What is stopping you from completing that risk?

_____
_____
_____
_____

_____
_____

During this week, you are going to take all three of your risks. Then, reflect on the following:

- Which one was easiest? Hardest?

- What surprised you about taking that risk?

- What was the outcome?

- Would you take that risk again?

Risk 1 Reflection

_____
_____
_____
_____
_____
_____
_____
_____
_____

Risk 2 Reflection

_____
_____
_____
_____
_____
_____
_____
_____
_____
_____
_____

Risk 3 Reflection

_____
_____
_____
_____
_____
_____
_____
_____
_____

Embracing Wild Impulses Safely

Risk-taking often gets a bad rapport, but it is actually one of the best ways that you can propel yourself forward. Now, you not only know how you can embrace your wild side through intelligently managed risks, but you also know how those risks can benefit you and anyone you lead. Next up, we are going to examine innovation and strategy, and why your wildness proves to be an unpredictable excellence in that area.

Chapter 5:

The Dance of the Unpredictable—

Innovation and Strategy

Do not follow where the path may lead. Go instead where there is no path and leave a trail. –Muriel Strode

Being unpredictable is a talent and skill. Wild women are often unpredictable, and for many people who witness this, it can be quite shocking. At the same time, wild women are known as beacons of unpredictability that lead to innovation and strategy, especially in the course of leadership. Let's find out how you can embrace your wild nature for unmatched innovation and strategy!

Women and Unpredictability

Women are known for being unpredictable. Where men would typically do something the same way every time, or they would apply the same methods to new concepts, women approach the world with a vision—one that is entirely unique every time. Understanding the inherency of the connection between women and unpredictability can be powerful for harnessing that trait in leadership.

Why Women Are Unpredictable

What is it about women that makes us so unpredictable? Is it the hair? The fashion? The vibes? None of the above! Women are unpredictable for several reasons, and all pertain to our natural instincts and interactions with the world around us:

- **Emotional connection:** Women tend to emotionally collect differently than men do, with stronger connections or increasingly profound connections being common. This leads to outcomes that are considered with care yet innovation.

- **Social factors:** Women naturally face a lot of social factors that lead to us having to make innovative decisions and overcome challenges. Combined with our natural propensity for novel social tactics, this can lead to unpredictable yet incredibly innovative understandings.

- **Gender-based conflict/stereotype:** Because of some of the intrinsic stereotypes that say us women socialize in certain ways, are over-emotional, or are otherwise "lesser than," we have developed a knack for handling conflict in innovative ways.

- **Disadvantages:** Disadvantages due to gender gaps and prejudice have forced us to come up with creative solutions to gender-related problems in order to catch up.

As you can see, women have a natural propensity for being unpredictable. And while many people will paint that negatively, we girls know the secret—it is a superpower. Now, it is time to learn how to use it!

The Connection: Unpredictability and Innovation

Unpredictability naturally gives way to innovation. Those who are spontaneous, impulsive, and unpredictable tend to produce the most original, creative, and fascinating solutions to problems, thinking outside of the box in ways that those who follow a cut-and-dry pattern of thinking would not come up with. This is specifically because those who are spontaneous are not self-conscious of their thoughts, free to try and fail and try again until they are confident and empowered.

And a wild woman is nothing if not spontaneous and confident. In your life, you have probably been given countless reasons to think, *Wow, what a stupid idea* about thoughts that were your very own. A workplace meeting might have left you silenced when it came to sharing ideas—what if you said something embarrassing or dumb? But as a wild woman, it is time to push that thinking away.

Wild women are bursting from the seams with innovation due to their unpredictability—something forged from the ashes of stereotypes and discrimination to create something all new: wild, unpredictable women with wonderful ideas. As a wild woman, your unpredictability leads to innovation due to a deep-seated refusal, whether inherent or newfound, to let your ideas be called stupid or shunned.

In all, your unpredictability as a wild woman creates innovation because of bold and courageous decisions paired with quick thinking, a fierce attitude, and unparalleled intellect. You have the ability to come up with ideas *and* implement them thanks to your wildness, and as a leader, this is something you want to use.

Embracing Unpredictability for Creative Problem Solving

"So," you are probably asking, "how *can* I use my unpredictability as a leader?" The answer lies in using that unpredictability for problem-solving—something every leader manages on a daily basis. Now, it is time to learn how your unpredictability can feed unique problem-solving talents.

Benefits of Unpredictability

First, however, we have to tuck into the benefits of unpredictability. With a firm understanding of the benefits of unpredictability, you will better grasp the scope of how unpredictable plus wild equals greatness.

One of the biggest benefits that leaders can gain from being unpredictable is the fact that no one can take advantage of them if they do not know their next move(s). This applies whether you head a company in a competitive market or lead a family, or anything in between. Unpredictability means that your virtue of creative problem-solving will always have you five steps ahead *and* that you will be able to counter the response from "enemies," so to speak.

Furthermore, unpredictability helps you avoid stereotypes as a leader. "We can talk over her because she never stands up for herself" quickly becomes "it is best to let her speak her mind fairly; you never know her next moves." This hones a sense of respect when it comes to you and your decision-making process. Someone who does not know what to expect will be forced to respect your process or get left in the dust.

As a leader, unpredictability also garners interest. People who have an unpredictable, yet responsible leader are more easily compelled to pay attention and give their time to someone, learning about their unique perspectives on a situation.

Aspects of Creative Problem Solving

With the benefits of unpredictability in mind, you can successfully exude strategy and innovation simply by knowing the aspects of creative problem-solving and how they intersect with that unpredictability. Some important aspects of creative problem-solving include

- **Balancing logic with creativity:** Creative problem-solving is harnessed by understanding how creativity intertwines with logic during the problem-solving process. Logic is a springboard that allows creatives to come to appropriate solutions.

- **Asking questions:** Creative problem-solving revolves around a strong tenacity for asking questions. When you ask questions, you have more to work with in terms of alternatives, planning, and more. Beyond that, some of the most creative solutions stem from asking, "What would happen if...?".

- **Deferring judgment:** In order to creatively solve problems, it is also vital to avoid letting judgment impact your process. Not all ideas will be good ones, but that does not mean that judgment is helpful. Therefore, while feedback is valuable, pointless judgment should be ignored.

- **Caring about the audience:** Lastly, creative problem-solving comes from caring about the audience and their perspectives. By considering the differing points of view of your audience, a creative solution can be synthesized together—making everyone happy in the process.

And with these aspects in mind, it becomes easy to know how to solve problems with creativity and unpredictability!

Embracing Creative Problem Solving Through Unpredictability

But if it is not obvious just how the two should be methodically used, let's talk about it. When you go to solve a problem, there are a lot of elements at play, as mentioned in the last section. You have balance, questions, avoiding judgment, and empathy. While these are all components that might make you feel restricted in spontaneity, they can actually help the process!

Being unpredictable does not mean being reckless. Part of never letting someone know your next move is always using different strategies and tactics to get the fiercely calculated results that you are known for. You can do this while balancing logic with creativity, for instance, by considering creative solutions and then testing them against logical outcomes.

Moreover, creative problem-solving through unpredictability hinges on being able to share your wildest ambitions without worrying about whether people think you are being silly or shooting too high. Rather than defending yourself in the fire of someone criticizing you, simply give them the understanding that it is not okay to judge people. A simple "I hardly think that statement was appropriate" can go a long way!

Unpredictable Strategizing: Military-Grade Wildness

Leading as a woman is a lot like being a fearless military commander at war. You have to manage so many inputs at once, overcome so many different conflicts and crossing strategies, and more, leaving your hands more than full when it comes to leading. With that being said, you also need to harness your ability to strategize with unpredictability to truly keep others on their toes.

Strategizing is the process of devising a course of action that will get you or your team closer to a goal. Naturally, this goes along with problem-solving because strategizing is how you put those problem-solving methods into action. Therefore, you can work with unpredictable strategizing by considering efficiency, empathy, and what you can do that is different from last time.

Wild Dreams, Golden Geese

Many women are taught to think that their wild dreams and ideas are not plausible. We are told that our ambitions are better kept to dreams and that the suggestions we make will not truly work. Because of this, it is easy for a woman to believe that her wild dreams are nothing more than a farce. But the reality of the matter is that your wildest dreams can be like golden geese.

How Wild Ideas Can Be the Best

In fact, sometimes, the wildest and "out there" ideas are the ones that work the best, have the highest efficacy, and trump other ideas altogether. But why is it the case that wild ideas can be the best? In my mind, it is simple. If an idea is not wild, then it has probably been done over—and over—and over again. It is played out and stale, which means that you need something new.

Enter the wild idea. The wild idea is something that has never been done before, especially not in the exact way that you plan to execute it. It is something no one sees nor has expected, yet here it is, ready to glimmer and shine. And wild ideas are not just the best because they are new; they are also the best because they are formed with passion.

This means that regardless of the personal connection, you likely created or formulated your wild idea with some care and consideration for it or your outcomes. That is more than people who recycle old ideas and call them new can say! Your wild dreams are laden with gold due to that unparalleled wild woman passion brewing within.

How to Embrace Your Wild Ideas

Embracing those wild ideas so that they can truly flourish and take hold involves letting go of what others think of you and your ideas. Every woman on this planet has allowed someone to tamp down their dreams and stop them from achieving greatness. As a wild woman, you have no time for this!

Instead, when someone criticizes your idea, you can take a few paths. Explain why that is not okay if you think they meant no harm. But if they were doing so with the strict intention of tearing you down, then it is time to consider an alternative method—and no, not violence! Rather, curtly inform them that you will not tolerate that treatment of yourself or anyone on your team.

Moreover, do not allow subconscious self-judgment to take hold. Ask yourself how you would respond if a teammate suggested the same idea you are admonishing, and see if the way you are treating yourself is then truly fair.

Wild Woman Rituals

You know the drill by now! These wild woman rituals will help you exercise your unpredictability and the power it has to help you truly embrace innovation and strategy as a leader.

Creative Solution Journaling Prompts

Coming up with creative solutions is easy—until you are on the spot. Use the following journaling prompts to help you come up with creative solutions using your natural unpredictability:

- Describe a problem you are currently facing. Now, reverse engineer the situation and brainstorm backward to identify potential solutions.

- Think of your problem as a metaphor (i.e., a tangled knot, a locked door). What creative solutions can you derive from this metaphor?

- Imagine you have traveled to the future, and the problem is already solved. What innovative solutions did the future you come up with? Describe them in detail.

- If your problem were a character in a story, what other fictional character or historical figure would you bring in to collaborate on a solution? How would their unique traits contribute to solving the problem?

- Consider the issue from the perspective of someone completely different from yourself (a child, an alien, a historical figure). How might they approach and solve the problem?

- Pick a random object around you. How can the characteristics or functions of that object inspire a solution to your problem?

- Reflect on your recent dreams. Are there any symbols or scenarios that could be metaphorically linked to your problem? How might dream-inspired elements lead to creative solutions?

- Draw or doodle your problem and then transform it into an abstract piece of art. What ideas or solutions does the artwork suggest?

- Think about how nature might solve a similar problem. Draw parallels between your issue and processes in nature. What can you learn from the natural world?

- Create a dialogue between different aspects of yourself, each representing a different perspective on the problem. How might these internal voices collaborate to find a solution?

- Embrace a constraint or limitation related to your problem (i.e., budget, time). How can this limitation lead to a more creative and resourceful solution?

- Imagine your problem as a sequence of scenes in a movie. Create a storyboard illustrating various steps toward resolution. What creative twists can you introduce?

Confidence Affirmations for Unpredictable Innovation

As you know, affirmations are powerful for cementing strong thoughts of confidence and pride. Some affirmations that you can use relevant to the chapter include

- I am a resilient and creative force, ready to navigate the unknown with confidence.

- My unique perspective and ideas bring a fresh and innovative approach to any challenge.

- I trust in my ability to adapt to uncertainty and turn it into an opportunity for growth.

- My creativity knows no bounds, and I am capable of finding solutions in the face of unpredictability.

- I embrace change as a natural part of the innovation process, and I am confident in my ability to thrive in new environments.

- I am a trailblazer, unafraid to explore uncharted territories and pioneer new ideas.

- My intuition is a powerful guide, leading me to innovative solutions that others may not see.

- I welcome challenges as opportunities to showcase my strength, resilience, and ingenuity.

- Confidence is my companion as I navigate the dynamic landscape of innovation.

- I trust in my capacity to learn and grow, recognizing that each challenge is a chance to expand my skills.

- I am a beacon of inspiration, encouraging others to embrace uncertainty and tap into their creative potential.

- My confidence is grounded in the belief that my ideas have the power to shape the future.

- I celebrate my successes, no matter how small, as they fuel my confidence and motivation for future innovations.

- I radiate self-assurance, inspiring those around me to approach unpredictability with courage and optimism.

- My innovation journey is a testament to my resilience, creativity, and unwavering confidence in my ability to make a positive impact.

Brainstorming Mini-Guide

Finally, it is important to know how to brainstorm ideas for when that innovation can feel a bit evasive. Your quick-start guide to brainstorming is as simple as these steps:

1. **Define the problem clearly:** Clearly articulate the problem you are trying to solve. Ensure that everyone involved in the brainstorming session understands the challenge.

2. **Set a positive and open atmosphere:** Create a comfortable and open environment that encourages creativity. Foster a positive attitude and communicate that all ideas are welcome.

3. **Establish clear goals:** Set specific goals for the brainstorming session. What do you want to achieve? Having clear objectives helps guide the creative process.

4. **Encourage divergent thinking:** Encourage participants to think broadly and come up with as many ideas as possible. Avoid judgment during the initial idea-generation phase.

5. **Use creative warm-up exercises:** Start with warm-up exercises to get creative juices flowing. This could be a quick association game or a brief mind-mapping activity related to the problem.

6. **Leverage different perspectives:** Invite people with diverse backgrounds, skills, and perspectives to the brainstorming session. Different viewpoints can lead to more creative solutions.

7. **Combine and build on ideas:** Encourage participants to build on each other's ideas. One idea can spark another, leading to the development of more innovative solutions.

8. **Utilize visualization techniques:** Use visual aids such as charts, diagrams, or drawings to represent ideas. Visualizing concepts can stimulate creative thinking.

9. **Embrace "Yes, and" thinking:** Instead of shutting down ideas, practice "Yes, and" thinking. Acknowledge and build upon ideas, even if they initially seem unconventional or unrelated.

10. **Take breaks:** Allow for short breaks during the brainstorming session. This can refresh participants' minds and encourage a new wave of creative thinking.

11. **Combine analog and digital tools:** Use a mix of analog tools like whiteboards and sticky notes, as well as digital tools for collaboration. This provides flexibility and accommodates different preferences.

12. **Encourage wild ideas:** Do not be afraid to explore wild or seemingly impractical ideas. Sometimes, the most unconventional solutions lead to breakthroughs.

13. **Prioritize and refine ideas:** After generating a significant number of ideas, prioritize and refine them based on feasibility, impact, and alignment with your goals.

14. **Test and iterate:** Implement a prototype or test the most promising solutions on a small scale. Use feedback to refine and iterate on the ideas.

15. **Celebrate and reflect:** Celebrate the successful brainstorming session and reflect on the process. What worked well, and how can you improve future brainstorming sessions?

With your newfound knowledge and intrinsic skills of innovation, you have everything it takes to be a powerful yet unpredictable force in the line of leadership. Now, it is time to shift our view to how you can build up your unbreakable tribe.

Chapter 6:

Tribal Rhythms—Building and

Nurturing Your Tribe

Encourage, lift, and strengthen one another. For the positive energy spread to one will be felt by us all. For we are connected, one and all. –Deborah Day

Wild women are known for their unwavering independence, but being independent does not mean that you have to do it all alone. In this chapter, you'll uncover the secrets to being a wild woman with a support network—making you a more unstoppable force than ever when you have your supportive tribe by your side.

The Value of a Tribe

Many women try to brave the world alone, without a supportive friend or a companion to back them up in sight. While you can certainly take this approach to life, you miss out on so much by not having a support network. You do not get the experiences, advice, recognition, or care that someone with a support network—something I like to call a tribe—does. Let's understand the value of a support network and what supportive people look like—together.

Why Support Networks Matter

Everyone needs a support network, but that is especially the case for a wild woman. We have so many factors working against us already, and a support network can make everything so much easier to bear. Some of the values of a support network include

- **Emotional support:** Support networks are your first line of defense when it comes to emotional support. When you are going through a hard time—anything from self-doubt to a tragic event—a support network is there to help you carry the load. This means that it becomes far easier to manage troubling emotions when you have a support network, as well as that you do not have to let those emotions impact your life in inappropriate ways.

- **Advice:** Sometimes, seeing something from a different perspective can make it easier to understand and manage. That is no different when it comes to the advice and diverse perspectives that your support network can offer. When you have a supportive tribe by your side, it becomes less of a challenge to deal with things on your own; you have your tribe to help you out, either literally or through advice.

- **Confidence boost:** Having a tribe is also a bit like having your own personal cheerleaders. A tribe is a group of individuals who lift one another up no matter what, being honest and considerate of each other. This ties directly into confidence, as having individuals who support you can be uplifting.

- **Connection and solidarity:** It can be helpful just to know that we are not alone in this world and that there are plenty of people willing to support us. That is another main function of identifying your own tribe.

And that is just the start of it. But at the same time, it is important to know that not everyone is supportive, even if they talk themselves up as though they are.

Understanding if Someone Is Supportive

One unfortunate fact of life is that not everyone we think is supportive will be truly and unequivocally supportive. Someone you consider to be supportive might become jaded and unsupportive; others might solely support you when it benefits them. This is not a testament to your worth, but rather a testament to their treatment of others. With that being said, it is important to learn how you can identify someone who is supportive.

Different people are supportive in different ways, but some of the common traits that all supportive people exhibit include

- **Active listening:** Someone who is supportive will not pretend to listen to you while they plan out their next meal or activity. Instead, they will actively listen to everything that you have to say to them, offering support and encouragement if needed.

- **Empathetic:** Supportive people are empathetic. They consider what you might be going through and how it would impact you, as well as anything they need to truly support you emotionally and as a companion. Empathy comes naturally to the supportive person.

- **Available:** "Sorry, I cannot" is not one of the top phrases of a supportive person. Someone who is truly supportive will, within reason, be able and willing to make time for you to support you and engage with you meaningfully.

- **Encouraging:** A supportive person will always encourage you to try new things, do what is best for you, and otherwise improve your life. When you experience success, they will celebrate; when you have a setback, they will help. Supportive people are encouraging no matter the context.

- **Reliable:** Supportive people are the ones that you can count on to be there for you. They follow through on plans and commitments and do not change who they are from one moment to the next.

- **Respectful:** A supportive friend will respect who you are, your decisions, and your boundaries. You will not feel unable to confide in a supportive individual because their support and willingness are vocal.

- **Helpful:** Supportive friends are ones who have the ability to be helpful when you need it most. They are unafraid to offer the support you need and go out of their way to help you during your times of need.

- **Communicative:** You do not have to beg for communication when you have supportive people by your side. True members of your tribe will be willing to communicate openly and honestly without hesitation.

- **Nonjudgmental:** Last, but certainly not least, your tribe of support will never judge you. That is because supportive people exercise acceptance and understand diversity, so they do not feel the need to put others down.

Finding Your Tribe

After hearing about the benefits of being surrounded by a strong tribe, as well as what members of a support network can be like, you are probably wondering how you can find a tribe of your own. It can be daunting at first, but slowly, finding your tribe becomes easy as pie.

Asking for Support

Finding your tribe can be easy if you know where to look and that begins with asking for support. A lot of wild women feel as though asking for support undermines their confidence and ability, but that is not the case at all. In fact, asking for help and support is a sign of strength; it is an act laden with vulnerability and courage, which means that wild women should feel empowered to ask for help.

Asking for support can be scary; therefore, it can be helpful to start small. Ask for small favors or instances of support, which will give you a window into who is and is not a good choice for support. Over time, you can build up to bigger instances of support. I also recommend asking directly if someone is willing to be in your support network—and thus have you in theirs as well. This transparency and confidence secures a connection and keeps everyone on the same page.

That brings me to my next point as well: Do not try to get someone to support you if you are not willing to support them in return. A support network is not a stepping stone to a goal; it is a group that helps make your life more fulfilling and encouraging. Therefore, everyone needs to support everyone, even if it is inconvenient or not personally beneficial.

At the same time, not everyone is responsible for you, nor do they have to go out of the way for you. While a supportive person will, not everyone is going to be right for your tribe or supportive toward you—and that is okay. It is not a reflection of you or your worth. Sometimes, people do not have the resources to help in the ways you need, and other times, people are worth your time. That said, do not feel like you cannot ask for support just because the first dart you throw does not stick.

They Do Not Always Have Matching T-Shirts

It can be tempting to look for your support network among your existing family and friends. After all, those who you are already close with are probably close for a reason. However, you cannot always expect that closeness is the same as support. Plus, taking a look outside of your immediate circle can expose you to supportive individuals you have not even met yet, fostering connections and fulfillment in the process.

With that in mind, it is important to know that not everyone in your tribe will be wearing matching T-shirts. You might find your tribe outside of your friends or family—becoming friends with coworkers, acquaintances, mutual friends, or even strangers. You can find supportive people in unexpected places or places you have never even looked! Some ideas for reaching out to others include

- **Online forums:** Online forums can be an insightful place to gather support from people who know just what you are going through. Whether you are a parent, teacher, manager, CEO, or anything in between, there is a forum online that can help connect you to supportive individuals.

- **Talk to the loners:** At work, school, or even more generally in life, there are going to be people who keep to themselves. And while introverts exist, a lot of people keep to themselves due to a lack of support. Even introverts need support, so try talking to those who keep to themselves and see if a connection can form.

- **Ask for support from the unsupportive:** Sometimes, we do not get the support we need from those in our lives, but it is not because they do not care. Some people genuinely do not know how to support a strong, wild woman, so it does not hurt to ask explicitly for the type of support that you are looking for.

- **Ditch the toxicity:** It can be hard to have strong bonds and get the support you need when you are constantly surrounded by toxic people who put you down. By shedding toxic people who do not care about your well-being, you become more approachable to supportive people while making time and space for them in your life.

- **Start the process:** Do not be afraid to extend support first. This can spark a chain reaction where people are kind and supportive of one another, ultimately improving your quality of life and chances of getting support.

And speaking of reaching out, you have to learn to be comfortable with taking chances and reaching out for support. Know your worth, but do not let this stop you from finding joy in the supportive hands of others.

Warmth: Inclusivity and Diversity

At the same time that you garner support from others, it is important that you be a supportive individual as well. Diverse communities, including women, often get overlooked, especially by leadership. This means that as a wild yet empathetic leader, you have the power to start an atmosphere of support by opening your arms to diverse individuals and being inclusive as a leader.

How You Can Support Diverse Individuals

Diversity comes in many shapes and sizes. As a leader, you may encounter sprawling and even unfamiliar elements of diversity where religion, gender, sexuality, age, ability, and more are considered. At the same time, supporting diverse individuals is crucial for creating inclusive and equitable environments.

The good news is that you have many options for supporting diverse individuals as a leader and being inclusive toward dynamics other than your own. Some of those methods include

- **Cultivate inclusive leadership:** It is important to demonstrate your commitment to diversity and inclusion through your decisions and actions as a leader. This means that not only do you have to harness an understanding of individual backgrounds, but an appreciation for different perspectives and opinions. By cultivating inclusive leadership, it sets the tone for your organization, family, or team to follow suit.

- **Educate and raise awareness:** As a leader, you have a unique role in educating your team. Everyone should have diversity and inclusion training to increase their awareness and understanding of unique situations. Encourage ongoing education about different cultures, backgrounds, and experiences to foster a team that does not just tolerate inclusion, but embraces it.

- **Promote equal opportunities:** It's not enough to encourage knowledge about diversity, especially if that does not have practical applications for those under your leadership. In other words, it is crucial that your team members have equal access to opportunities for growth, development, and advancement regardless of circumstances. This includes addressing and eliminating hiring, promotional, and assignment-based bias.

- **Flexible work practices:** Where possible, do not be afraid to implement flexible policies that can accommodate diverse needs, such as remote work options, flexible hours, and parental leave. Such policies make it easier for disabled workers, new parents, and other groups to participate in your team's dynamics. Also, consider different cultural practices and religious observances when planning schedules and events so that the customs of individuals can be honored.

- **Celebrate diversity:** Make it a point to celebrate diversity through cultural events, recognition programs, and awareness campaigns. You can invite individuals to share their culture through workplace events, for instance, allowing others to appreciate, accept, and admire other cultures.

- **Address microaggressions and bias:** Microaggressions may not seem like much to someone who is not targeted by them, but to someone who is, it is an impactful sign that their diversity is not respected. Include sensitivity training and genuine reprimanding for those who engage with microaggressions to show that they are not tolerated.

Beyond that, you can go above and beyond by ensuring that no one feels excluded. This can be as simple as being mindful around the holidays that there are diverse celebrations, or as complicated as advocating for a coworker who is being treated unfairly. Your inclusion and diversity-tolerant attitudes are nonnegotiable in a supportive environment!

Wild Woman Rituals

Of course, we cannot forget about a few wild woman rituals that help you navigate what you've learned.

"Are They Supportive?" Quiz

It can be hard to tell when someone truly supports us. You might think that someone supports you, only to find out that when your back is turned, they are brandishing a knife. This quiz will help you gauge whether someone is actually a supporter, or if it is time to drop them like it is hot.

1. How often does your friend make time for you when you need to talk or share your thoughts?

2. Has your friend rearranged their schedule to support you in times of need?

3. Does your friend actively listen to you without interrupting?

4. Does your friend show an understanding of your perspective, even if it differs from their own?

5. Does your friend provide positive reinforcement and encouragement in your pursuits?

6. Does your friend react positively when you face challenges or setbacks?

7. Can you depend on your friend in times of need?

8. Is your friend consistent in keeping commitments to you?

9. Does your friend respect your need for personal space and privacy?

10. Does your friend respond well when you set boundaries?

11. Has your friend actively assisted you in achieving your goals recently?

12. Is your friend willing to lend a helping hand without expecting anything in return?

13. Does your friend support you when you are going through difficult times?

14. Does your friend show empathy and understanding during challenging situations?

15. Does your friend react positively when you achieve a significant milestone?

16. Is your friend genuinely happy for you when you succeed?

17. Is your friend approachable when you need to discuss sensitive topics?

18. Does your friend handle difficult conversations while maintaining a supportive attitude?

19. Has your friend engaged in any random acts of kindness for you recently?

20. Does your friend contribute positively to your well-being?

Naturally, you can replace "friend" with whatever dynamic you have. You can score them based on the following and how many "yes" answers you tally:

- **15+:** Supportive person with a few exceptions, but everyone makes mistakes!

- **10–14:** They try to be supportive but might need to be told how they can best support you.

- **7–9:** Somewhat supportive, but not really someone you want to be in your tribe as a main member.

- **6 or fewer:** This person is not really supportive of you or only supports you when it is convenient for them.

Journaling: I Feel Supported When...

Journaling is a magnificent way to help you understand what you need to feel supported. Take some time to write down your responses to questions like

- When was the last time I felt fully supportive?

- What signs tell me that someone is a supportive person?

- What does it mean for me to feel supported?

- How do I show other people support?

Overall, having people who support you can make life easier. You have people who can help you grow into the best version of yourself all while having a few laughs and some good memories to enjoy. Being with your tribe is a feeling like none other, and now it is one that you can embrace.

Chapter 7:

The Howl at the Moon—Resilience

and Fighting Spirit

The most common way people give up their power is by thinking they don't have any. —Alice Walker

Wild women have to take the time to howl at the moon, let their hair down, and release a few battle cries. Something about wild women is that we never back down, which means that we often find ourselves in the midst of chaos. This is where resilience and the need for a fighting spirit intersect—something you will learn all about in this captivating chapter.

Understanding Resilience

Resilience is of the essence for any powerful, wild woman. This is specifically because being a wild woman is not an easy job to fulfill. As a wild woman, you have intersecting struggles of being judged, underestimated, and more, making it hard to bounce back from anything from a bad comment to a failed plan. At the same time, resilience is one of the most important skills for success, so let's ensure that you have it.

Understanding Resilience

But wait—what is resilience in the first place? Simply put, resilience refers to our ability to bounce back. Someone who can perceive a failure as a learning experience without missing a beat is something who excels in the field of resilience. You might think you are resilient enough, but when something gets you down and that interferes with your ability to be a boss-like woman, it becomes strikingly apparent that resilience is something you are lacking.

Fortunately, everyone can develop resilience, and it only takes a few small skills. Mainly, resilience relies on being confident and self-assured. Someone who is resilient has an unwavering mentality of confidence that coincides with their ability to employ a growth mindset—something I have mentioned before yet have not explored in depth.

A growth mindset is the opposite of a fixed mindset. A growth mindset refers to a mindset where one believes their skills, talents, and traits to be honed, improved, and developed; a fixed mindset is akin to believing that whatever traits you were born with are the best traits that you will have. Naturally, a growth-focused mindset leads to more improvement due to a belief that you can improve.

This type of mindset is what wild women who want to get far develop. Throughout the course of this chapter, you will find elements that lend to helping you engage that growth-focused mindset that will leave you empowered and able to bounce back from anything that comes your way.

Resilience and Gender

Did you know that, statistically speaking, women tend to be far more resilient than men (*Are Women More Resilient than Men?*, 2023)? And I'm not just saying that; women tend to score higher on various indicators of resilience than men do time and time again. This means that in many regards, we have a natural ability to bounce back from the negative—we just have to learn to embrace it.

But why are women more resilient in the first place? There are many lines of thought that explain this apparent difference between men and women. For example, many professionals believe that women have higher levels of resilience because they are able to form stronger emotional connections with others. This enforced connection to others can boost our confidence and ability to come back from struggle.

Furthermore, it may be the case that women are more resilient because we are more able to express our emotions openly, which contributes to emotional exploration and awareness. In turn, we can process our emotions faster and come to resilient conclusions with ease, thus aiding in the process of overcoming challenging feelings as well. Because society frequently tells men to *avoid* emotional expression, they can be at a disadvantage when it comes to emotional resilience.

Even though we may be more naturally resilient, it is not an easy process to develop your own sense of resilience from the ground up; however, you need not worry! I have some handy tips to improve your resilience as a leader—after we explore why leaders need resilience in the first place.

The Value of a Resilient Leader

Being resilient as a leader is important for your personal well-being; however, that resilience also extends into your ability to lead with honor and dignity. There are many reasons that a leader should have resilience, especially considering that the attitudes and mentality of a leader trickle down to their team. Some reasons that you as a leader need resilience include

- **Overcoming setbacks:** As a leader, you will undoubtedly face countless setbacks. You can either bounce back and improve, or you can let that setback be your complete and utter downfall. Chances are, as a leader, you'll want the former to be your reality. That's something that you achieve through none other than our friend resilience.

- **Empathizing with the team:** Resilience is closely linked with the skill of empathy, which means that by being a resilient person, you can empathize with those on your team far better. This makes you a more respected leader who members are not afraid to come to.

- **Setting an example:** Being a resilient leader means that you are setting a positive example for those you lead. This means that every member of your team will be more readily able to handle conflict and struggles thanks to the example you put forward.

- **Keeping the team calm:** In stressful times, your resilience will be able to keep your team calm and collected.

And more. Being a leader is more than just commanding—it is also about the way others perceive you and how that perception shapes them as a team.

Steps to a More Resilient Mind

Cultivating a resilient mindset only takes five key steps:

1. **Cultivate a positive mindset.** A positive mindset is fundamental to unmatched resilience. Even in challenging times, it is important to remain focused on the positive. Not only can this be done through the development of a growth mindset, but you can do this with gratitude, too. Focus on the aspects of a situation that are in your favor, thus allowing you to have a mindset more directed toward resilience.

2. **Build strong relationships.** In order to be resilient, you then need to focus on fostering supportive connections with family, friends, and more. This means that you should seek emotional support when needed, as well as offer support to others in order to help them be more resilient as well. Social connections are an invaluable facet of resilience because they provide a buffer during difficult times.

3. **Develop problem-solving skills:** Resilient leaders are ones who know how to solve problems like a pro. Make it a habit to break larger challenges into smaller and more manageable tasks. Then, you can identify practical steps that will help you solve your problem and approach those problems with a solution-oriented mindset.

4. **Care for your physical and mental health:** Individuals who are resilient take the time to care for their physical and mental health, which is especially important. With weak physical and mental health, you will not be able to bounce back.

5. **Be adaptable and flexible:** Lastly, you have to master the art of being adaptable and flexible so that anything that comes your way is able to be resolved or managed aptly.

Turning Setbacks Into Comebacks

A final major component of resilience that you need to keep in mind is turning setbacks into comebacks. When you face a setback, you can either let it truly set you back, or you can use it as an opportunity to get ahead and do better next time. This means that resilience is based on using setbacks as an opportunity to come back.

In order to do so, you need to acknowledge the setback and accept that it has happened. Do not be resistant to the fact that a setback has occurred if you want to overcome it. Reflect on the experience to find out what did not work and why it did not work. Once you can figure that out, you have already done half the work!

Then, using your five steps to resilience, you can create a strategic plan to do things differently the next time. Between experience and logic— something wild women can synthesize for flawless progress—you have everything you need to then turn a setback into the comeback of a lifetime.

Drawing the Fighting Sword

Now for the moment you have been waiting for—the fight. We wild women need action, energy, and passion. You have probably been wondering how and when that would come into play—how you can encourage your wild, slightly aggressive, and otherwise unrelenting nature as a leader. Well, that is what this section is for—teaching you to be wild while emotionally powerful all in one.

Are Women Over-Emotional and Prone to Overreacting?

One of the biggest stereotypes that we face as women is the idea that every strong emotion we have is overreacting or us being overly emotional. Is that truly the case, or is this all a big social misunderstanding? Let's talk about it.

There are two popular lines of thought regarding the "do women overreact" debate:

1. **Yes:** Women overreact because we have strong emotions and are told by society—whether directly or implied—that reacting "normally" gets us looked over.

2. **No:** Women are told we overreact because it is an easy way to subdue us.

There is evidence, first-hand support, and more for each thought, so really, I believe it is up to you personally to judge whether you overreact or are overly emotional (Morin, 2019).

However, I do not believe that female-typical overreacting is anything to be ashamed of. Just like I have encouraged you to consider the diversities of others, it is important to recognize the diversities of yourself. Overreacting as a woman or being especially sensitive is not something to look down upon; it is a superpower. With that said, you have the ability to embrace your superpower wholeheartedly and use it while brandishing your fighting sword.

Standing Up for Yourself vs. Aggression

As women, it is no surprise that we are going to have to stand up for ourselves and what we believe in. That is especially the case for a woman in a leadership position. Because it can be easy to get spoken over or disrespected, you have to know how to successfully confront, manage, and defeat stereotypes, microaggressions, and other forms of subtle "putting women down" behaviors.

And I will let you in on a secret: Standing up for yourself is far different than being aggressive. You might feel like you cannot stand up for yourself because if you do, then you are being aggressive. That is simply not the case, no matter what others may try to make you feel like. Standing up for yourself is not aggression because standing up for yourself involves a different skill called assertiveness.

Earlier in the book, we talked about what assertiveness is and how you can be assertive. Being assertive involves speaking up for yourself, calmly refusing to let others walk all over you, and otherwise being firmly rooted in self-advocacy. Aggression, on the other hand, can involve seeming threatening or menacing to command others. Typically, aggressive leaders are viewed as unable to compromise, unempathetic, and ruthless.

Is Aggression Ever Warranted as a Leader?

Hearing about aggression as a concept, you might think that you have to avoid aggression altogether; however, you can choose to embrace aggression as one tool in your toolkit as a wild woman. Being aggressive can be balanced with compassion if you play your cards right, which can result in a leader who has the ability to assert dominance while still knowing when to pull back.

Your Inner Warrior-ess: When to Pull Out the Fighting Sword

As a wild woman in leadership, you have to know when and how to wield that fighting sword for the best results. Doing so involves a careful balance of confrontation, wisely placed aggression, a competitive edge, and emotional regulation.

Calculated Confrontation

The point of confrontation is two-fold; it is meant to raise awareness of something and put someone on edge. Confronting someone for bad behavior does this just like confronting someone in a competitive way does. In order to pull out that fighting sword, it is important to balance cooperation with confrontation. Every interaction need not be a confrontation, but when confrontation is needed—such as to defend yourself or someone else—you should be comfortable doing so boldly.

Using Aggression Wisely

If you use aggression as a tactic, be sure to use it wisely. Aggression is a tactic that works best when paired with empathy and used in moderation, so do not be afraid to use aggression as a secret tactic for only the most severe cases.

Tapping Into Competition

Competitiveness is another tool that can help you wield the fighting sword with honor. Being competitive as a leader is a great skill to have, specifically because it encourages friendly competitors to better themselves and strive for more. You can tap into competition personally by encouraging others to challenge you in a friendly way or offering competitions that encourage it.

Emotional Regulation

At the same time, it is important that you can regulate your emotions. This does not mean suppressing your wild nature, nor does it mean conforming to the emotional standards that others set for you. Emotional regulation simply refers to keeping your emotions in check—measured against a personal standard—so that they do not impact your ability to do your job and be an empathetic leader.

Wild Woman Rituals

Welcome to your wild woman rituals! It is time to put your fighting spirit and resilience to practice with these exercises.

Affirmations: A Confident Fighter

Even the most confident of fighters can appreciate a few affirmations. Be sure to put these into use by chanting them in the mirror, howling them at the moon, or just thinking them to yourself before stepping into the office:

- I am a strong and capable leader, and my voice deserves to be heard.

- I trust my instincts and make decisions with confidence and clarity.

- My unique perspective brings valuable insights to every situation.

- I am resilient and capable of overcoming any challenges that come my way.

- I am deserving of success and will not shy away from opportunities.

- I lead with authenticity, embracing my true self in every role I take on.

- I am not afraid to take risks and step outside of my comfort zone.

- My confidence inspires and uplifts those around me.

- I am a trailblazer, paving the way for other women in leadership.

- I trust my abilities and know that I am well-equipped to handle any situation.

- I celebrate my achievements and acknowledge my contributions to the team.

- I am bold, powerful, and fully capable of achieving my goals.

- I stand tall in my convictions, unapologetically expressing my ideas.

- I radiate confidence, and others are drawn to my leadership style.

- I am a leader who empowers and supports those around me, fostering a positive and inclusive environment.

The Resilience Worksheet

Next up, a worksheet to help you practice resilience! Fill out the worksheet whenever you feel yourself struggling with resilience, ideally somewhere where you can reflect on your journal entries often.

Date: _____

List three past challenges or setbacks you have faced in your leadership journey.

_____
_____
_____
_____
_____
_____

_____
_____
_____

Reflect on how you responded to each challenge. What strengths did you demonstrate?

_____
_____
_____
_____
_____
_____
_____
_____

Identify three personal strengths or skills that have contributed to your success as a leader.

_____
_____
_____
_____
_____
_____
_____
_____
_____

How can you leverage these strengths during challenging times?

_____
_____
_____
_____
_____
_____
_____
_____

Describe a recent experience where you embraced a growth mindset and learned from a setback.

_____
_____
_____
_____
_____
_____
_____
_____
_____

How can you apply a growth mindset to future challenges?

_____
_____
_____
_____
_____
_____
_____
_____
_____

List individuals in your personal and professional life who provide support and encouragement.

_____
_____
_____
_____
_____
_____
_____
_____
_____

Develop three positive affirmations that resonate with your journey as a female leader.

_____
_____
_____
_____
_____
_____
_____
_____
_____

Being a resilient, powerful wild woman is not hard when you have the right skills in your toolkit, and now you do! Next, it is time to zoom in on the empathy and kindness women do best, forging a spot for those skills within your dynamic as a leader.

Chapter 8:

The Untamed Heart—Empathy

and Intuition in Leadership

Intuition is the discriminate faculty that enables you to decide which of two lines of reasoning is right. Perfect intuition makes you master of all. –Paramahansa Yogananda

Intuition and empathy are a dynamic duo that any wild woman should be familiar with. I can say that, in many ways, these skills come more naturally to women; however, wild women often feel or are expected to negate empathy and intuition, especially in the context of leadership. But empathy and intuition are powerful catalysts of success, connection, and power for leaders, and this chapter will help you master the art of balancing your fierceness with empathy and balancing your logic with intuitive powers.

Trusting Your Intuition

Intuition is something that everyone has to some extent, but not everyone chooses to take advantage of it or hone their abilities to be intuitive. At the same time, intuition can amplify your ability to make responsible decisions as a leader, especially where logic isn't so cut and dry.

More Than a Late Night Burrito: Understanding Intuition

Intuition is more than just a late-night burrito that causes an upset stomach and an "off" feeling. It is a powerful tool that can be harnessed to improve knowledge, decision-making, and interpersonal interactions. Intuition refers to our ability to just know something, without the need for cognitive reasoning or logic. You might intuitively know that someone isn't a good person or that an idea will fail, even without thinking about it or having evidence.

Many people underestimate intuition, but it can actually be quite powerful. Intuition isn't always right, but then again, neither is logic. In certain situations, trusting your intuition is more fruitful than thinking about it logically! Some intuition-craving situations you may encounter include

- **Safety:** Intuition can help us know when we're at risk of danger. You should always trust your intuition when it comes to safety, like leaving a situation when you feel the need to or putting safety measures in action.

- **Health signals:** Intuitive health signals pertaining to the body should always be listened to as well; they highlight important changes you need to make for physical well-being.

- **Something is "off":** If you feel like a person or situation is just "off," it's a good time to listen to your intuition. Even if you aren't going to act right away, filing that intuitive suspicion is helpful.

- **Doubt:** If you intuitively know something, trust that. Your doubt may try to overpower your intuitive knowledge, but don't let it.

But where does our intuition come from? It's not like intuition comes from the kidneys or something. Well, intuition actually comes from the brain, and much like logically parsing through a decision-making process, intuition leafs through everything you know to come to a conclusion. When you think of something intuitively, it's because your brain has almost instantaneously gathered that knowledge from your past experience and knowledge, presenting it to you directly.

Knowing that, it's clear that intuition is something of a superpower. Intuition helps you know something without having to truly think it over, resulting in instantaneous judgments and understanding. With that in mind, let's uncover the benefits of intuition.

Benefits of Intuition

On average, we make upwards of 35,000 decisions a day (Marples, 2022). For wild women, leaders, and wild women who lead, this number is probably much higher. If you spent time treating each of these decisions as individual decisions without using your intuition, you'd spend all day doing what you already get done by 8 a.m. With that being said, your intuition is invaluable as a leader. Some of the functions of intuition for leaders include

- **Speed:** Using intuition to make decisions naturally speeds up the process. Intuitive decisions can be made almost immediately, and even if logic is needed, you can work from the basis of an intuitive decision to make a logical one, laying the groundwork in a split second. As a result, you have the ability to make more powerful decisions faster. This can be especially helpful for leaders who frequently have to make snap decisions.

- **Empathy:** In order to use intuition, you have to be in tune with the emotional landscape, at least a little bit. This means that your intuitive decisions are somewhat based on emotions as well, thus leading to a more empathetic leader. Those who lead with intuition are more emotionally fair to their team and are able to consider the emotional consequences of a decision.

- **Risk assessment:** Though it may seem like favoring intuition is a risky choice on its own, intuition can actually help when it comes to the art of risk assessment. Your intuition has the power to let you know almost immediately whether a decision is going to be risky, and even how risky that decision may be. This is invaluable for wild leaders!

- **Creativity:** Intuitive decisions are spontaneous, which means that they almost always have an added touch of creativity that you can't find elsewhere. This means that you can come up with more creative solutions that actually work, all thanks to your powerful intuition.

Being an intuitive woman and leader is like having a superpower and competitive edge wrapped up in one. And the best part is that everyone has intuition and everyone can improve theirs!

Are Women More Intuitive?

Some people think that women are far more intuitive than men or that women have a natural knack for intuitive judgment. But is this really true, and if it is, what does it mean for you as a wild woman? Let's discuss!

I'll go ahead and answer the main question you have—are women more intuitive? The answer: not necessarily. Women and men seem to have a similar tenacity for intuitive skills, which means that we're on a pretty level playing field as far as inherent intuitive abilities go. However, studies show that women actually practically use their intuition far more than men do (Bao et al., 2022).

So, what does this mean? It means that while men can be just as intuitive as women, they choose to go the route of deliberative thinking more than intuitive thinking. In turn, women have more practice with their intuition and can wield it more effectively in leadership positions. Alongside men, we have the ability to make a decision-making tag team that is infallible—but for now, let's focus on you.

Tips for Trusting Your Intuition

Alright, so you have an empowered background on intuition and what it is. How can you then move into trusting your intuition and strengthening it, as opposed to approaching it with an attitude of doubt? Some ways that you can work to trust your intuition more as a wild woman in leadership include

- **Know yourself.** Cultivate self-awareness. Reflect on your experiences and decisions to understand your intuition better. What patterns do you notice? What tendencies guide your instincts?

- **Become an expert.** Deepen your knowledge and expertise in your field. The more you know, the more informed your intuitive decisions can be. Blend your intuition with a solid foundation of information.

- **Embrace diversity.** Actively seek input from various sources. Your intuition benefits from considering diverse perspectives. Create an inclusive environment that values and welcomes different viewpoints.

- **Take calculated risks.** Trusting your intuition involves taking risks. Be open to stepping outside your comfort zone. Understand that intuition plays a role in navigating uncertainty, and sometimes, risks lead to the best outcomes.

- **Reflect regularly.** Practice mindfulness and reflection. Connect with your inner thoughts and feelings. Regular moments of introspection help you stay attuned to your intuition.

- **Build your support network.** Surround yourself with mentors, advisors, and colleagues who provide feedback. A reliable support network helps validate or challenge your intuitive insights.

- **Balance logic and intuition.** Recognize when to rely on data-driven decisions and when to trust your instincts. Striking a balance between logic and intuition is crucial for effective decision-making.

- **Never stop learning.** Hone your intuition through continuous learning. Embrace opportunities for growth and development. Exposure to different situations refines your intuitive capabilities.

- **Listen to your gut feelings.** Actively listen to your gut feelings. Trust your initial reactions and explore the reasons behind them. This allows for a deeper understanding of your intuition.

- **Create a positive environment.** Foster a positive and supportive work environment. Trust and express your intuition without fear of judgment. A culture that values intuition contributes to your effectiveness as a leader.

- **Be adaptive.** Embrace adaptability. Your intuition thrives in an environment where you can adjust strategies based on changing circumstances and feedback. Adaptability is key to successfully incorporating intuition into your leadership practices.

By taking the time to steadily practice intuitive abilities, you will become a better leader, teammate, and wild woman. You've got this!

Wild Woman's Guide to Empathy

Along with intuition, it's important to be an empathetic leader and wild woman. A lot of people think wild women can be quite abrasive, so it becomes your job to prove them wrong! Empathy involves understanding and profoundly considering the emotions of others. As a leader and wild woman, this skill is invaluable.

The Value of Empathetic Leaders

Being an empathetic leader is important for many reasons. In a world where people are unnecessarily nefarious toward one another, empathy is more important than ever, especially in the workplace. Empathetic leaders make some of the best leaders because

- Empathetic leaders build strong and positive relationships with their team members. Understanding and acknowledging the feelings and perspectives of others fosters trust and camaraderie.

- Empathy promotes effective communication. Leaders who empathize can better comprehend the needs and concerns of their team, leading to clearer and more open communication.

- When leaders demonstrate empathy, they show that they care about the well-being of their team. This, in turn, boosts morale and motivation. Team members are more likely to be engaged and committed when they feel understood and supported.

- Empathetic leaders excel in resolving conflicts. By understanding the emotions and motivations of those involved, leaders can address underlying issues and find solutions that satisfy all parties.

- Employees appreciate leaders who show empathy. Feeling heard and valued contributes to job satisfaction. Empathetic leadership creates a positive work environment, leading to higher levels of contentment among team members.

- Empathy fosters a culture where diverse ideas are acknowledged and respected. Leaders who understand the unique perspectives of their team members are more likely to encourage innovation and creativity.

- Empathetic leaders are better equipped to adapt to change. By understanding how change impacts individuals, they can navigate transitions more effectively and guide their team through challenges.

- Employees are more likely to stay with a company where they feel understood and supported. Empathetic leadership contributes to higher employee retention rates and fosters loyalty within the team.

- Empathy is not limited to internal relationships. Leaders who understand and empathize with their customers can better meet their needs and build lasting relationships, ultimately benefiting the organization.

- Empathetic leaders consider the ethical implications of their decisions. Understanding how choices impact individuals allows leaders to make decisions that align with values and principles.

How to Embrace Empathy

Now, you're probably wondering how you can embrace empathy as a wild woman in leadership. Leading with empathy is a powerful and transformative approach, especially for women in leadership roles. In a world that often emphasizes strength and assertiveness, embracing empathy sets you apart, fostering meaningful connections and driving positive change within your team and organization.

As a woman in leadership, you can recognize the diverse perspectives within your team to foster empathy. Empathy starts with understanding the unique experiences and challenges that each team member brings to the table. Take the time to listen, appreciate, and acknowledge the richness that diversity adds to your team. Furthermore, stand up for the diverse individuals on your team by showing kindness and consideration, even if you don't necessarily understand their choices or perspectives fully. Allowing diversity to root within your team heightens your empathy and the empathy that teammates show for one another.

In addition, try to connect with those on your team in a personal sense. Show genuine interest in the lives of your team members. Understand their aspirations, struggles, and motivations. By doing so, you create a space where individuals feel seen, valued, and understood. This also fosters a sense of closeness and trust within your dynamic. You can do this by asking questions, encouraging casual conversation in the workplace (or within your home if you lead as a mother), and making time for your team to come together and conversate.

Furthermore, it's a good idea to create an environment where your team feels comfortable expressing their thoughts and concerns. Be approachable and open to feedback. Empathetic leaders foster a culture of trust, enabling team members to share their ideas and challenges without fear of judgment. Whether you're a mom or a company owner, being open and approachable means that people will trust and confide in you, express themselves, and overall work to improve the team, thanks to the precedent that you've set.

Additionally, empathy extends to supporting the growth of your team. Understand the aspirations and career goals of each individual. Provide opportunities for skill development and advancement. Your investment in their growth demonstrates not only empathy but a commitment to their success. Beyond that, make sure that you provide individuals with the opportunity to grow in a personal sense thanks to their time with your leadership—something that can apply to any team circumstance.

Empathy in leadership also has to do with how you handle challenges. In leadership, challenges are inevitable. Leading with empathy means navigating these challenges with compassion. Understand the impact that difficulties may have on your team and offer support. By showing compassion during tough times, you build resilience and loyalty within your team. And empathy isn't just reserved for challenging moments— it's equally important during times of celebration. Acknowledge and celebrate the achievements of your team. Taking the time to recognize and applaud successes reinforces a positive and supportive work culture.

By being an empathetic leader, people will look up to you and your wildness with fond admiration. Some of the most iconic female leaders are those who lead through empathy, so don't be afraid to let your softer side out to play every now and then.

Wild Woman Rituals

It's time for a few more wild woman rituals, this time focusing on journaling and decision-making using the powers of feminine intuition.

Intuitive Journaling

Journaling can be a powerful tool to help you develop and strengthen your intuitive abilities. Follow the directions below to hone your intuition through normal journaling:

1. Set aside dedicated time each day for intuitive journaling.

2. Before you begin, take a few deep breaths to center yourself.

3. Reflect on a specific question or situation you are currently facing. It could be a personal or professional decision, a challenge, or anything that requires insight.

4. Write down your initial feelings, thoughts, and any subtle impressions that come to mind without overthinking.

5. Pay attention to any recurring themes, symbols, or patterns in your journal entries over time.

6. Periodically review your entries to observe how your intuition evolves and whether it provides valuable insights.

7. Share your experiences and reflections with a trusted friend or mentor for additional perspectives.

Intuitive Decision-Making

You likely use logic to make most of your decisions, with emotions coming in second. But how often do you tune into your intuition alone to make decisions? Chances are, very rarely! For this activity, simply follow these steps to get some practice with intuitive decision-making:

1. Choose a relatively simple decision you need to make, such as what activity to engage in during your free time or what to cook for dinner.

2. Before analyzing the options logically, take a moment to close your eyes and focus on your feelings about each choice.

3. Pay attention to any gut feelings, instincts, or intuitive nudges that guide you toward a particular option.

4. Make your decision based on the intuitive insights you receive.

5. Reflect on the outcomes of your decision and how they align with your initial intuitive impressions.

6. Gradually increase the complexity of decisions you make using intuition, moving from simple choices to more significant ones.

7. Keep a record of your intuitive decision-making experiences and assess the accuracy and impact of your intuitive choices over time.

Intuition and empathy are like a dynamic duo that contributes to your ability to interact with others while balancing the blunter side of being wild. Now, you have everything you need to balance those two sides of yourself!

Chapter 9:

Running With Wolves—

Collaboration and Community

It is literally true that you can succeed best and quickest by helping others to succeed.
—Napoleon Hill

For any wild woman, collaboration and taking advantage of the benefits of community is vital. We have a lot going against us due to social perceptions, but united, we are stronger than ever. In this chapter, you'll find out exactly how we can work together, form a sense of community, and avoid negative conflict.

Collaboration for the Pack

Any wild woman needs the ability to collaborate *and* to encourage those around her to collaborate. By understanding the value of collaboration and discovering how you can be a more collaborative leader, you can amplify your wild woman powers even further.

Why Collaboration Is Valuable

As a leader, people are going to do what you do—if you're mean, they will be too, and if you're kind, so will they be. That said, you have to set the stage for collaboration first so that everyone else is able to follow you. But why does collaboration matter in the workplace? It's because

- When you foster collaboration, you open the door to a wealth of diverse perspectives and ideas. Your team is likely composed of individuals with unique skills, experiences, and viewpoints. By encouraging collaboration, you tap into this diversity, gaining insights that can lead to innovative solutions and well-rounded decision-making.

- Collaboration strengthens the bonds within your team. It creates an environment where team members feel heard, valued, and part of a collective effort. A cohesive team, where individuals collaborate seamlessly, is more resilient in the face of challenges and adapts more effectively to change.

- As a leader, you encounter complex challenges. Collaboration brings together minds with different strengths and expertise, resulting in more robust problem-solving. The collective intelligence of your team is a powerful asset that can be harnessed through collaboration to navigate even the most intricate issues.

- In today's fast-paced world, innovation is key to staying ahead. Collaboration nurtures an environment where creativity flourishes. By encouraging your team members to share ideas, experiment, and learn from one another, you create a culture of innovation that can drive your organization forward.

- Employees are more engaged and motivated when they feel a sense of purpose and connection to their work. Collaboration provides them with opportunities to contribute meaningfully, work together on projects, and feel a sense of ownership. This, in turn, leads to increased job satisfaction and a more dedicated team.

- Change is inevitable, and effective collaboration positions your team to adapt more smoothly. When individuals collaborate, they share the responsibility of navigating change, making the process less daunting. This agility is a hallmark of successful leadership in today's dynamic business landscape.

- As a leader, your behavior sets the tone for the entire team. When you actively engage in collaboration, you model the behavior you expect from others. Your commitment to working collaboratively fosters a positive culture that encourages teamwork and mutual support.

In essence, collaboration is not just a strategy; it is a mindset that can transform your leadership approach. By embracing collaboration, you elevate the capabilities of your team, inspire innovation, and create an environment where everyone can thrive. As you embark on your leadership journey, remember that your success is intricately tied to the collaborative spirit you cultivate within your team.

Putting Your Collaboration to the Test

Becoming a wild woman with a propensity for collaboration is simple! It involves

- **Embrace your authentic leadership style.** Your authenticity is your strength. Embrace your unique leadership style, leveraging your strengths and values. Authenticity fosters trust among your team, laying the foundation for a collaborative environment where everyone feels comfortable contributing their ideas.

- **Cultivate active listening.** Listening is the cornerstone of effective collaboration. Actively listen to your team members, seeking to understand their viewpoints. By demonstrating genuine interest, you create a space where individuals feel valued, encouraging open communication and collaboration.

- **Promote inclusivity.** Make it a priority to create an inclusive environment where diverse voices are not only heard but celebrated. Actively seek out perspectives from team members of different backgrounds and experiences. Inclusivity fosters a richer collaborative dynamic that fuels creativity and innovation.

- **Build strong relationships.** Invest time in building strong, authentic relationships with your team. Understand their aspirations, challenges, and motivations. A leader who values personal connections fosters a sense of belonging, enhancing collaboration as team members feel more comfortable sharing their insights.

- **Encourage collaborative problem-solving.** Instead of providing all the answers, encourage your team to participate in problem-solving. Facilitate collaborative discussions where different perspectives are considered. This not only leads to more robust solutions but also empowers your team members to take ownership of their work.

- **Acknowledge and celebrate achievements.** Recognize and celebrate the accomplishments of your team. A collaborative leader acknowledges the contributions of each team member, reinforcing a sense of shared success. This positive reinforcement fuels a collaborative spirit and motivates your team to continue working together effectively.

- **Provide opportunities for skill development.** Foster a culture of continuous learning and growth. Provide opportunities for your team members to develop new skills and expand their expertise. This investment in their professional development not only benefits individuals but also enriches the collaborative capabilities of the entire team.

- **Lead with empathy.** As a woman leader, empathy is one of your greatest assets. Understand the unique challenges faced by your team members, and show empathy in your leadership approach. A leader who understands and supports their team fosters a collaborative culture built on trust and compassion.

Conflict Resolution: When the Wolves Fight

Conflict is unavoidable as a leader. Members of your team are going to have conflicts from time to time, either among themselves or with you. Understanding conflict and how to manage it is an instrumental talent all wild women need.

Types of Conflict

Did you know that there are many different types of conflict? Not all conflict is built equally, so it is important to be able to discern between conflict types. In a setting where you lead, there are a few conflicts that you will be most familiar with:

- **Interpersonal conflict:** Conflict occurring between two or more individuals as a result of differences in personalities, communication styles, or values. This often occurs for leaders as two team members fight or they argue with someone themselves.

- **Intergroup conflict:** Conflict occurring between two different groups. You may experience this if you lead a company, for example, as two groups compete.

- **Intragroup conflict:** Conflict that arises within a particular group. This can happen over tasks, responsibility, or decisions that members disagree on the treatment of.

- **Cultural conflict:** Conflict arising from differences in cultural backgrounds, norms, or values. Misunderstandings or clashes between individuals from diverse cultural backgrounds are common examples of cultural conflict.

- **Value-based conflict:** Conflict stemming from differences in core values, beliefs, or ethical principles, such as disagreements on organizational values and conflicts related to ethical decision-making.

By understanding the difference between conflict types, you can take a unique approach to each one—setting the stage for unique resolutions and even prevention moving forward.

Conflict Can Be Positive

There is this idea that floats around that conflict is only negative. Conflict does not always have to involve people who are angry at one another and ready to tear each other apart; not only can conflict be peaceful, but it can also come from a place of well wishes and a desire to strengthen a team. I am letting you know this so that you don't feel like all conflict has to be shut down immediately. Letting your team work together to solve a problem can actually be beneficial in myriad ways.

For example, conflict resolution encourages the team to get closer to one another. And a team that can work well together is a team that will withstand any storm that comes their way. Beyond that, resolving conflict where others are involved can improve the creativity of your team members, helping them understand how to be tolerant of the ideas of others. In turn, this improves the strategic thinking skills, collaborative abilities, and diversity of thought within your team.

As you can see, conflict does not have to be a bad thing just because it involves a handful of people who disagree. Conflict can be a powerful catalyst for self-improvement and team strengthening, leading to a team that wants to work with one another instead of against another.

Conflict Management Tactics

Helping out with conflict management is a piece of cake for any wild woman with the right skills—and those skills include

- **Cultivating open communication:** Encourage a culture of open dialogue within your team. Create a space where team members feel comfortable expressing their concerns and opinions. By fostering transparent communication, you lay the groundwork for resolving conflicts proactively.

- **Assertive communication:** Embrace assertiveness in your communication style. Clearly express your thoughts and expectations while respecting the perspectives of others. A balance of assertiveness and openness sets the tone for constructive discussions.

- **Active listening:** Actively listen to the concerns of your team members. Demonstrate genuine interest and empathy, acknowledging their feelings and viewpoints. A leader who listens fosters an environment where individuals feel valued and understood.

- **Collaborative problem-solving:** Involve your team in the resolution process. Collaborative problem-solving not only taps into the collective intelligence of the group but also empowers team members, making them feel invested in finding solutions.

- **Addressing issues promptly:** Don't let conflicts linger. Address issues promptly and directly. Timely intervention prevents the escalation of conflicts and demonstrates your commitment to maintaining a positive work environment.

- **Embracing flexibility:** Be flexible in your approach to conflict resolution. Recognize that different situations may require different strategies. Your ability to adapt and tailor your approach showcases agility and a keen understanding of your team dynamics.

- **Promoting inclusivity:** Ensure that all voices are heard and valued. Actively seek perspectives from diverse team members. Inclusivity not only enriches decision-making but also promotes a sense of fairness and equality within the team.

- **Leading by example:** Model the behavior you wish to see in your team. Demonstrate how to handle conflicts with professionalism, empathy, and a focus on solutions. Your actions set the standard for collaborative behavior.

- **Providing constructive feedback:** When conflicts arise, offer constructive feedback. Focus on behaviors and actions rather than personal attributes. Constructive feedback helps individuals understand the impact of their actions and encourages positive change.

- **Investing in team building:** Proactively invest in team-building activities. Strengthening interpersonal relationships creates a foundation of trust, making it easier to navigate conflicts when they arise. Team cohesion is a powerful tool in conflict prevention.

Raising Wild Women

Lastly, it is important that you contribute to helping other women be wild. Two particularly simple yet effective ways that you can do so is through inspiring others to be themselves and sticking up for unique individuals.

Inspiring Others to Be Themselves

Part of raising up wild women and promoting wildness in others involves inspiring others to be themselves. A lot of wild women become subdued or even temporarily lose their wildness due to the judgment of others. This means that they need to be encouraged to come out of their shell, and women who are already wild need to defend and reinforce that being wild is okay. In order to have that, other wild women like yourself have to inspire such a thing.

You can encourage other wild women to be themselves by simply being yourself with unwavering confidence. But if you want a more hands-on approach, you can even share some of the exercises or readings from this book with them. You can also inspire them by encouraging silliness, like asking, "What would be the craziest idea to solve this problem," during team conversations. And, of course, don't let anyone with something against us, radiant wild women, trample over the wildness of your teammates and colleagues.

Outside of that, you can help other women feel wild by explaining why wildness is a good thing. If one of your members is behaving particularly wildly, don't be afraid to say to them, "Yes! I love that idea and your enthusiasm!" Such a response only encourages that wildness to continue.

Sticking Up for Others

Of course, wildness is not always received well—this is something that you and I know better than anyone. Being wild is often frowned upon for many reasons, and while you may now have the confidence to embrace being wild anyway, not all women have reached that level just yet! It is important that you take the time to uplift other wild women by standing up for them—and, in return, letting others stick up for you.

You can stick up for others in many ways, but the best way to do so is by using your position as a leader. If you see someone being mistreated for any reason—be it appearance, personality, culture, or anything else—step in and let the person mistreating them know that that is not okay. If you are in the position to, provide relevant punishments for those taunting, teasing, or bullying others—because, yes, adults face this as well.

Wild Woman Rituals

I hate to say it, but it is time for our final wild woman rituals of the book. These activities focus on helping you improve conflict resolution and collaboration on a personal level.

Conflict Resolution Prompts and Questions

As a leader, you probably will not go a day without conflict of some sort. The following questions can help you ritually resolve conflict by asking open-ended questions that solve problems without "ordering" or seeming "bossy" as two people work to resolve a situation:

- What seems to be the main source of conflict in this situation?

- Can you identify the specific issues or concerns raised by each party involved?

- How long has this conflict been ongoing, and has it escalated recently?

- Have you taken the time to actively listen to each individual involved in the conflict?

- What emotions or underlying concerns are being expressed by each party?

- How can you demonstrate empathy and understanding to those involved?

- Are there any misunderstandings or miscommunications that may have contributed to the conflict?

- Can you help clarify expectations or roles to ensure everyone is on the same page?

- What information might be missing that could provide a clearer picture of the situation?

- What are the common goals and objectives that all parties share?

- How can you align individual goals with the overall objectives of the team or organization?

- Are there compromises that can be made to find a mutually beneficial solution?

- How can you encourage open and honest communication between the parties involved?

- Are there effective communication channels in place, or do they need improvement?

- What strategies can be implemented to foster a culture of transparent communication?

- Have you considered different conflict resolution models or strategies?

- What steps can be taken to de-escalate tension and promote a positive resolution?

- Are there external resources or mediators that could assist in the resolution process?

- How can you promote a positive and inclusive team culture to prevent future conflicts?

- What team-building activities or initiatives can strengthen relationships within the team?

- Are there opportunities for professional development to enhance interpersonal skills?

- What measures can be implemented to monitor the resolution and prevent a recurrence of the conflict?

- How will you follow up with the individuals involved to ensure that the resolution is effective?

- Are there lessons learned that can be applied to improve conflict resolution processes in the future?

Collaboration Quiz: Where I Can Improve

And now for a quiz! Answering these questions and analyzing your answers will help you understand where you can improve your collaboration-based skills as a leader:

1. When working in a team, I prefer

    A. Taking charge and making decisions.

    B. Collaborating and sharing decision-making with the team.

    C. Following instructions and completing assigned tasks.

2. In a group project, how do you usually handle conflicts or disagreements?

    A. Assertively express my opinions and try to convince others.

    B. Seek compromise and find common ground with team members.

    C. Avoid conflicts and hope they resolve themselves.

3. How do you contribute to group discussions?

    A. Speak up frequently and share my ideas.

    B. Listen actively and contribute when I have valuable insights.

    C. Prefer to observe and only speak when directly addressed.

4. When working on a collaborative document, how do you handle feedback from others?

    A. Defend my ideas and resist changes.

B. Consider feedback and make revisions collaboratively.

C. Implement feedback without discussion to get the task done.

5. In a team setting, how do you handle differing work styles among team members?

   A. Encourage everyone to adapt to my preferred work style.

   B. Adapt my work style to accommodate diverse preferences.

   C. Work independently to avoid conflicting work styles.

6. How do you approach sharing credit for a successful project?

   A. Ensure that my contributions are highlighted.

   B. Acknowledge the collective effort of the team.

   C. Downplay my role to avoid attention.

7. When faced with a challenging task, how likely are you to seek input from others?

   A. Rarely, I prefer to tackle challenges on my own.

   B. Sometimes, if I think others can offer valuable perspectives.

   C. Always, I believe collaboration enhances problem-solving.

8. How do you handle deadlines in a collaborative project?

   A. Focus on my tasks, and assume others will do the same.

   B. Communicate regularly to ensure everyone is on track.

C. Trust that the team will meet the deadline without my involvement.

Here is your scoring key:

- For every (a) response, give yourself 1 point.

- For every (b) response, give yourself 2 points.

- For every (c) response, give yourself 3 points.

And your interpretations for each score:

- **8–12 points:** There is room for improvement. Consider focusing on enhancing your collaboration and teamwork skills.

- **13–18 points:** You have a moderate level of collaboration skills. Identify specific areas for growth and build on your strengths.

- **19–24 points:** Well done! You have strong collaboration skills. Continue to foster a collaborative mindset and share your expertise with others.

Being a wild woman is not a solo job; now, you can help uplift other wild women, facilitate positive interactions, and more. With these skills, you can make being wild look easy!

Chapter 10:

The Future Is Wild—Embracing

the Call of the Wilderness

The best way to predict your future is to create it. –Peter Drucker

Not too long from now, I expect that the future will be characterized by wild women. On every team, in every home, and during every conversation, people will search for a wild woman to diversify, lead, and change the game. We do it better than anyone else, and soon, the whole world will be able to embrace that. But for now, it is time for you to embrace the upcoming future where your wildness is not just accepted—it is encouraged.

The Future Is Wild

The future is wild. Wild women make so many unique contributions to society that it is a wonder why we are not in higher demand. Understanding how the future can be wild is a powerful way to understand, even on bad days, that your unique gifts and traits are needed.

The Impact of Wild Women

Wild women make a unique imprint on the world. In Chapter 1, I highlighted some of the famous wild women who you may admire or look up to, but what about us unsung heroes—those of us who do not have articles in *TIME* or a *New York Times* best-selling novel on the way? We matter, too! And to help you understand the power of the impact of wild women, we are going to discuss some hands-on examples of wild women making a difference that you can see in your own life.

Let's start with mothers. To be a mother is to inherently be a wild being. Most mothers carried a life around inside of them for nine months, and even mothers who adopt or foster have met their fair share of challenges and struggles to earn the title of mother. But beyond mere relation, mothers do so many things that grant them the title of wild:

- **Teach:** As a mother, you are a child's first teacher. That is not something to take lightly. Mothers teach skills ranging from speech to empathy and everything in between. It is because of mothers that children grow into intelligent, kind, and amazing human beings. That is not to say dads do not do some of the work, but nothing really matches the warm, inspiring lessons of a mother.

- **Grow:** Not only do mothers help their child grow, but a mom is constantly growing herself. Being someone's mom means that you have to constantly change to meet the dynamic of a family, which is not easy to do! Being a constantly changing individual, the rock and support pillar for a child is pretty wild to me.

- **Nurture:** All mothers nurture their child emotionally and physically. You ensure that they stay in good health, teach them emotional skills in a way no one else can, and provide selfless support to them even on your worst days. This nurturing mentality is definitely something I would say wild women have—wild women can be sensitive, too, you know.

- **Resolve:** Wild women who are also mothers certainly are not afraid to step into the danger zone when it comes to conflict. Conflict between a co-parent, two siblings, the school and one's child, and more are all a comfortable war zone wild moms can step into and resolve.

- **Fight:** Finally, wild moms are not scared by a little conflict. They will do whatever it takes, whenever needed, to keep their child safe, comfortable, and cared for, even if it means baring a grin in the face of danger.

Simultaneously, good and powerful mothers benefit society in an unmatched fashion. Wild moms raise wild children who then share those important traits with the world. Moreover, wild yet caring moms are more likely to impart wisdom, empathy, and other positive traits to their child, resulting in a more compassionate, kind society.

The next impactful wild woman role is that of the inventor. Wild women have ideas that no one else has. We see them every day as wild women patent inventions and share them in stores, online, and more. It truly takes someone wild to create an invention that changes lives—whether it is a new piece of gardening decor or something that makes life easier for marginalized groups. Investors are unarguably useful and desired, and wild women take the cake for some of the best.

Then, there are the managers, owners, and wild women in the workplace. These are the wild women who keep their heads up no matter what happens at work, effortlessly leading a team using skills both in and outside of this book. Naturally, female leadership is important for diversity, but at the same time, wild women lead immensely well.

So, how does all of this pertain to the future? It is simple—being a wild woman and encouraging others to embrace their wildness forges a future where these impacts and benefits are only increased. By being unafraid to show your wildness and hold the hands of other women as they learn to do the same, these impacts become broader and more widespread than ever.

The Bridging Gender Gap

On top of what I have just mentioned, there is some good news. While the gender gap is still present, strides are being made every day to bridge that gap. For example, from 2000 to 2004, women only made around 76.9% of what men made (Wulfhorst, 2021); today, women make around 83.7% of what men make (Chun-Hoon, 2023). While that gap has not closed much, it *has* closed—and is continuing to close.

Women's rights are a major conversation today, as women from diverse religions and cultures gain more and more rights—and when those rights are taken away, we have to stand up for one another. Female sexuality is becoming more and more accepted, and other strides are being made every single day. That said, we, as wild women, also have the ability to step in and fight for the rights of ourselves and other women—including those who cannot do so safely.

Women cannot fix everything purely on our own, especially in a society that is undeniably male-dominated in many ways; however, we do have plenty of options for contributing to bridging that gender gap, and wild women are just the people to do that. Some ways that you can contribute to bridging the gender gap include

- **Education and skills:** Women are just as capable of skill and intelligence as men, but many women are afraid or discouraged when it comes to seeking those traits out. As a woman, and a wild one at that, you can bridge the gender gap a bit by seeking out education yourself and encouraging others to do the same. In conversations, shut down "jokes" that women are unintelligent, and be sure to advocate for women to seek training in science, technology, engineering, and mathematics (STEM) subjects.

- **Mentorship and networking:** Women can play a crucial role in supporting each other through mentorship and networking—and wild women are able to share their wildness with others. Something that you can do is encourage the establishment of mentorship programs where experienced women guide those entering the workforce and can provide valuable insights and opportunities. Building a strong network of professional connections helps women access resources, share experiences, and create a supportive community.

- **Advocacy for inclusive policies:** It is important that you also actively participate in advocating for policies that promote gender equality in workplaces and communities. Support initiatives that address issues such as equal pay, flexible work arrangements, and parental leave. Advocate for these policies in political networks as well, especially through raising awareness and advocating for change.

Wild Woman Traits the World Needs More Of

I have said it before, and I will say it again: The future is wild. The world, then, needs more wild woman skills in order to adapt to the changing world and to better itself as a whole. The skills and traits of wild women are instrumental to a future where we as humans—as a society—are more kind, confident, and extraordinary.

Just a few of the wild woman-specific traits, things women like us do best, that society needs include

- **Communication:** Communication is just one of the many skills you have mastered over the course of this book, so you know by now just how amazing we can be at communication with the right skills in mind. Every day, people fight and argue needlessly, engage in conflict, and otherwise demonstrate a need for more effective communication. With the communication skills of yourself and other wild women, more peace can be attained.

- **Fierceness:** Wild women are naturally fierce, even if they are introverts. This fierceness means that wild women can stand up for themselves and their tribe without fail. If everyone had the ability to do that, then the world would be a more uplifting place—especially where leaders are involved.

- **Resilience:** We are not resilient just because we are wild; we are resilient because there is so much working against us already. Because of our unparalleled resilience, women can bounce back faster and stronger every time. This is a skill that everyone needs not just for the betterment of society, but for their own well-being, too.

- **Empathy:** So many conflicts could be resolved if people were just a little more empathetic toward one another. Empathy comes naturally to women, and even to those of us who had to learn it; it is a powerful skill we can teach. Empathy can save the world—I truly believe that—and it starts with us.

- **Connection:** I taught you how to find your tribe earlier. This connection is another wild woman skill that we can share with the world for profound improvement and relationship benefits.

By being a wild woman, openly and without hesitation, you have the power to gift these traits to society for a brighter future where people are kinder to others, kinder to themselves, and more powerful as leaders.

She Was Too Wild: The Highest Compliment

I can predict a lot of things about the future, and one of my predictions is that one day, "She was too wild" will be the highest compliment. Today, if someone says, "She was too wild," it is with a sour taste in their mouths. "Too wild" is synonymous with uncontrollable, impulsive, crazy—all things that those in leadership today are afraid of. But in the future, things will be different.

In the future, people will look at one another after you leave a room and say, "Wow, she was wild!" Wildness will be reimbursed with impressed attitudes and admiration. "Wild" will be synonymous with "incredible" and with employers wanting a wild woman on their side and friends of husbands commending them for what an amazing wife they have. Wildness will be nothing to be ashamed of in the future—if, and only if, you embrace your wildness and encourage others to do the same.

Being wild means not apologizing for it. There is a difference between being cold and uncaring as opposed to being wild; wild women are kind and empathetic, but unapologetically themselves. This means that you can safely embrace and promote your inner wildness completely and fully; promoting a society where wild women are the norm is perfectly safe and appropriate. We should encourage young girls, young adults, and even senior ladies to embrace this wildness.

And by setting the example yourself, people can take a look at what a confident, wild, and free woman looks like. As a leader, people look up to you, no matter if you lead a family or company. This means that the example that you set does rub off and that people who follow you or witness your leadership will mimic what you do in their own way. You can also play a direct hand in spreading wild behaviors and personalities, as we are about to discuss.

Embracing a Wild Future

Embracing a wild future means that there will be more people involved—those who compete with you and want to be like you. Learning how to manage the wildness of others, all while maintaining wildness as a lifestyle, can improve your ability to share wildness with others.

Interacting With Other Wild Women

During your time as a wild woman, you are going to encounter other wild women. These are not catty women who refuse to be civil no matter what; rather, they are women like you who are outspoken and endlessly passionate. You have mutual values and traits, which can be an amazing thing. This means that supporting your fellow wild women can be a wonderful opportunity to expand that tribe.

When you meet a wild woman, do not be afraid to reach out. Let her know that you admire her for what she does best, and do not be afraid to support her in social contexts. Let your wildness feed from each other's wildness, becoming more powerful and uplifting in the process. You do not have to be in contest with other wild women, because we naturally tend to work well together.

In the context of leadership, leading a team of wild women or being led by a wild woman is like being friends with your team. You have the ability to bounce ideas off of one another in a novel manner, without having to beg to be respected or ask to be accommodated for your communication, empathy, and energy. In essence, a group of wild women in a room together is powerful because of mutual understanding.

At the same time, sometimes matching personalities can clash. If you are on bad terms with a wild woman or have an altercation with her, just communicate. You have the powerful skills of empathy and communication, so you can certainly put them to use with other wild women. Engaging with wild women should not be a burden; it should be a chance to uplift one another.

Inspiring Others to Be Wild

As a wild woman and a leader, you are in the perfect position to inspire other women to be wild as well. And you do not have to do so just by being yourself. In other words, you can take hands-on, practical steps to encourage other women to be wild, including

- **Asking questions:** In leadership positions, asking questions can encourage others to toss ideas into the ring and speak their minds. This means that asking for opinions, allowing others to talk about how they feel about your leadership, and more can encourage an environment of openness and wildness.

- **Talking to the quiet ones:** Sometimes, the quietest people have the best ideas and are just afraid to express them. As a leader and empathetic wild woman, make it a point to ask the quiet members of your team how they feel. Get to know them and their perspectives, which will encourage openness among your colleagues and assert you as a safe, admirable leader.

- **Encouraging collaboration:** Rather than having everyone do their own thing, encourage people you lead to work together. Collaboration is more than beneficial when it comes to leadership scenarios, and besides, it is a wild woman's favorite skill when it comes to getting things done. Reward collaboration and find plenty of opportunities for it within your field.

- **Facilitating problem-solving:** As a leader, you are the main problem solver that everyone is going to look to. This means that you have the perfect opportunity to share your wild woman problem-solving skills with your team, encouraging both creative problem-solving and communication throughout the team as a result.

- **Rewarding spontaneity:** Allow your teammates to act with safe levels of spontaneity, thus encouraging them to engage with the creative process. Reward spontaneity by letting members know that you appreciate and notice their efforts, encouraging spontaneity to continue and benefit your tea.

- **Helping with risk-taking:** Use your wild woman skills to explain responsible risk-taking and promote it within the scope of your team. Guide your team through evaluating risks as you've encouraged them to do, and implement natural yet effective consequences that make a "failure" more of a learning experience.

- **Contributing to inclusion:** Be sure to promote inclusion so that others feel safe and comfortable demonstrating what makes them wild as well.

Being wild means that you have passion and drive, which can be put to use in starting a chain reaction of wild, free personalities thanks to your authority as a leader.

Being wild is nothing to be afraid of. One day, we will live in a future where "she was too wild" is the highest of compliments, and where everyone will strive to embrace the unique traits that make them wild. For now, the journey begins with you. This book is ending, but your exploration of your inner wildness is truly just getting started.

Conclusion

Leading as a woman is a uniquely challenging experience when considered among a landscape built for men. But now, you know that wild women have what it takes to embrace their wildness and become the best leaders around. The world is not always a place where wild women are accepted, which is why we have to push forward and build a place of our own—we deserve at least that much for ourselves!

To be a wild woman, you don't have to fit the Chapter 1 archetype to a T. In fact, you don't have to fit it at all! Whatever your personal definition of wild is, so long as you strive to be that in everything that you do, then you are a certifiably wild woman!

You don't have to feel shut down, trapped in a box, or like a puppet on show for others any longer. Now, you have everything it takes to be a fiercely wild woman and be the best leader possible, including

- An understanding of what it means to be a wild woman, paired with wisdom on how women have *always* made the best of the best when it comes to leaders.

- Why perfectionism is often forced onto women (and why your flaws make you an even better leader than a perfectionist).

- Communication 101: Never get spoken over again thanks to fierce conversational strategies that leave you heard, felt, and understood–without scaring away those who can't handle your wild, captivating personality.

- What calculated risks are and how you can make them, simultaneously demonstrating that a wild and sometimes reckless woman can achieve more than those who never take a risk.

- Bold and innovative strategies that leave you wild and unpredictable—all while maintaining that hallmark admirability of a memorable leader.

Underrated, wild women make the best leaders because we are not afraid to do what it takes to drive for success. There truly is no "I" in "team," and wild women know that better than anyone else. With the skills you have mastered across the course of this book, you are ready to unleash your rebel yell onto the world and be unforgivingly wild, embracing what it means to be you.

Get out there and live your life in accordance with this wild woman manifesto, never backing down to a "be quiet" command again. You are perfectly imperfect, wild, and free.

References

Agaragimova, E. (2022, May 10). *Women may make better leaders than men, science shows: feminine leadership qualities that drive success.* Training Industry. https://trainingindustry.com/articles/diversity-equity-and-inclusion/women-may-make-better-leaders-than-men-science-shows-feminine-leadership-qualities-that-drive-success/

Albright, M. (n.d.). *Madeleine Albright quote.* BrainyQuote. https://www.brainyquote.com/quotes/madeleine_albright_433588

Angelou, M. (n.d.). *Maya Angelou quote.* Goodreads. https://www.goodreads.com/quotes/700564-if-you-are-always-trying-to-be-normal-you-will

Bao, W., Wang, Y., Yu, T., Zhou, J., & Luo, J. (2022). Women rely on "gut feeling"? The neural pattern of gender difference in non-mathematic intuition. *Personality and Individual Differences, 196,* 111720. https://doi.org/10.1016/j.paid.2022.111720

Breaking barriers: influential women leaders from history. (n.d.). Emory University. https://ece.emory.edu/articles-news/breaking-barriers-influential-women.php

Chun-Hoon, W. (2023). *5 fast facts: the gender wage gap.* DOL Blog. http://blog.dol.gov/2023/03/14/5-fast-facts-the-gender-wage-gap#:~:text=Stats.

Coker, D. (2022, June 11). *Why men interrupt women—how do you handle interruptions at work.* The HR Digest. https://www.thehrdigest.com/why-men-interrupt-women-how-do-you-handle-interruptions-at-work/#:~:text=When%20men%20interrupt%20conversations%2C%20they

Day, D. (n.d.). *Deborah Day quote*. Goodreads. https://www.goodreads.com/quotes/557409-encourage-lift-and-strengthen-one-another-for-the-positive-energy

Drucker, P. (n.d.). *Peter Drucker quote*. BrainyQuote. https://www.brainyquote.com/quotes/peter_drucker_131600

Eliot, T. S. (n.d.). *T. S. Eliot quote*. BrainyQuote. https://www.brainyquote.com/quotes/t_s_eliot_161678

Females on average perform better than males on a "theory of mind" test across 57 countries. (2022, December 26). Neuroscience News. https://neurosciencenews.com/cognitive-empathy-females-22139/

Fleming, L. (2023). *When should you trust your intuition?* Verywell Mind. https://www.verywellmind.com/when-to-trust-your-intuition-7481322#toc-when-you-shouldnt-ignore-your-intuition

Hill, N. (n.d.). *Napoleon Hill quote*. BrainyQuote. https://www.brainyquote.com/quotes/napoleon_hill_385887

How do you develop your intuition as a leader? (2024). LinkedIn. https://www.linkedin.com/advice/0/how-do-you-develop-your-intuition-leader-skills-decision-making

Empathy in leadership: importance, benefits, & examples. (2023). Management Consulted. https://managementconsulted.com/empathy-in-leadership/#:~:text=Beyond%20developing%20personal%20connections%20and

Indeed Editorial Team. (2023). *What is an empathetic leader? (definition, benefits and tips to become one)*. Indeed Career Guide. https://www.indeed.com/career-advice/career-development/empathetic-leaders

Kimbarovsky, A. (2017, May 1). *How you can become a better leader by recognizing your own weaknesses*. Crowdspring Blog. https://www.crowdspring.com/blog/leaders-leadership-weaknesses-

mistakes/#:~:text=With%20weaknesses%2C%20leaders%20ar
e%20better

Lewis, O. (2023, April 7) *Women more likely to suffer from imposter syndrome than men, according to research*. The Independent. https://www.independent.co.uk/life-style/women-imposter-syndrome-workplace-confidence-b2313770.html#:~:text=A%20study%20of%204%2C000%20adults

Ma, B. L., Julie. (2022, February 2). *25 famous female leaders on power*. The Cut. https://www.thecut.com/article/25-famous-female-leaders-on-empowerment.html

Marples, M. (2022, April 21). *Decision fatigue drains you of your energy to make thoughtful choices. Here's how to get it back*. CNN. https://www.cnn.com/2022/04/21/health/decision-fatigue-solutions-wellness/index.html#:~:text=Whether%20you

Mayo Clinic. (2020, May 29). *Stressed out? Be assertive*. Mayo Clinic. https://www.mayoclinic.org/healthy-lifestyle/stress-management/in-depth/assertive/art-20044644

Morin, A. (2019, March 26). *Women really do apologize more than men. here's why (and it has nothing to do with men refusing to admit wrongdoing)*. Inc. https://www.inc.com/amy-morin/women-really-do-apologize-more-than-men-heres-surprising-reason-why-and-it-has-nothing-to-do-with-self-esteem.html

Myatt, M. (2010, September 7). *Leadership & perfectionism*. N2Growth. https://www.n2growth.com/the-need-for-speed/#:~:text=Leaders%20who%20fall%20prey%20to

New research shows women are better at using soft skills crucial for effective leadership and superior business performance, finds Korn Ferry. (2016). KornFerry. https://www.kornferry.com/about-us/press/new-research-shows-women-are-better-at-using-soft-skills-crucial-for-effective-leadership#:~:text=Women%20are%2045%25%20more%20likely

Novotney, A. (2023, March 23). *Women leaders make work better. Here's the science behind how to promote them.* American Psychological Association. https://www.apa.org/topics/women-girls/female-leaders-make-work-better

Prakashan S, H. (2023, March 13). *Are women more resilient than men?* Happiest Health. https://www.happiesthealth.com/articles/womens-wellness/are-women-more-resilient-than-men#:~:text=Several%20studies%20show%20that%20women

The rising need for empathetic leadership: 5 ways to lead with empathy. (2023). LinkedIn. https://www.linkedin.com/pulse/rising-need-empathetic-leadership-5-ways-lead-empathy-fuel50

The role of intuition in leadership decision-making: trusting your gut or overthinking it? (2023). LinkedIn. https://www.linkedin.com/pulse/role-intuition-leadership-decision-making-trusting-your-gut#:~:text=Here%20are%20some%20of%20the

Schroeder, H. (2022, January 17). *Great leaders trust their intuition.* SIGMA Assessment Systems. https://www.sigmaassessmentsystems.com/great-leaders-trust-their-intuition/

Strode, M. (n.d.). *Muriel Strode quote.* BrainyQuote. https://www.brainyquote.com/quotes/muriel_strode_101322

Trigger, B. G. (2003). *Family organization and gender roles.* Cambridge University Press; Cambridge University Press. https://www.cambridge.org/core/books/understanding-early-civilizations/family-organization-and-gender-roles/CD23A46C38F2C4ADCD9262CE0E107928#:~:text=Lower%2Dclass%20women%20in%20all

Trippeer, J. (2021). *Exploring female character archetypes.* Creative Screenwriting. https://www.creativescreenwriting.com/exploring-female-character-archetypes-the-wild-woman/

Walker, A. (n.d.). *Alice Walker quote.* Goodreads. https://www.goodreads.com/quotes/15083-the-most-common-way-people-give-up-their-power-is

Wulfhorst, E. (2021). *How the gender wage gap has changed over the last 40 years.* Assemble. https://www.assemble.inc/blog/how-the-gender-wage-gap-has-changed-over-the-last-40-years#:~:text=2000%2D2004%3A%20Women%20earn%2076.9

Yogananda, P. (n.d.). *Paramahansa Yogananda quote.* AZ Quotes. https://www.azquotes.com/quote/756259

Zenger, J. (2015). *Age, gender and ability to listen: who listens best?* Forbes. https://www.forbes.com/sites/jackzenger/2015/06/11/age-gender-and-ability-to-listen-who-listens-best/?sh=3b61fa299bf6

www.ingramcontent.com/pod-product-compliance
Lightning Source LLC
Chambersburg PA
CBHW070719130626
46553CB00005B/2065